How to Become a Successful Beauty Supply Storeowner

How to Become a Successful Beauty Supply Storeowner

By: Professor Devin Robinson

Going Against the Grain

Going Against the Grain Publications titles are published by:

Going Against the Grain Group

P.O. Box 44503

Atlanta, GA 30336

ISBN-13: **987-0-9842577-1-3**

ISBN-10: **0-9842577-1-3**

First Printing: April 2010

Printed in the United States of America

**Get the complete Beauty Supply System
<u>exclusively</u> at
<u>www.beautysupplysystem.com</u>**

Book available at:

<u>www.devinrobinson.com</u>

<u>www.amazon.com</u>

Table of Contents

ACKNOWLEDGEMENTS:

Thanks to: God for blessing me with the abilities to achieve and the ability to be a blessing to others.

Special thanks to: My family for dealing with the minimal communication we had while I was meticulously getting this endeavor together.

Thanks to my first employees, (ages at the time) my sons Devin Jr. (13), Dyshaun (9) and Damien (7), (ages at the time), for being the most affordable, trustworthy and hardworking employees an entrepreneur can ever ask for.

Thanks to both of my older brothers, Calvin and Kevin, for putting up with a brat little brother and for always encouraging me throughout the years to be above average and insisting that I believe in myself.

Thanks to my numerous family members, you are instrumental to me in our business endeavors and our *pursuit of happiness!*

Thanks to the stylists at my salon that came through in the clinch by giving me counsel on which products were most needed as I moved forward with opening my first store.

Thanks to all of the customers that saw the big picture and supported the stores even when we did not have everything they needed or when we were not totally competent in the details of the products, yet you kept coming back!

ABOUT THE AUTHOR:

Devin A. Robinson was born the great-great grandson of a runaway slave on St. Thomas, United States Virgin Islands. He grew up under the influence of two entrepreneur grandfathers and several entrepreneur uncles. He spent six years in the U.S. Army then returned to civilian life in 1998. He spent a short stint in the corporate world before returning to his roots of entrepreneurship.

Devin successfully opened three beauty supply stores within an 18-month period after being disrespected, threatened and ejected from an Asian-owned beauty supply store for no apparent reason. His operations are emulated in each store and have become the blueprint for the other aspiring storeowners he is continuing to help along the way.

Devin believes highly in the art of conducting business to a high standard and stops at nothing to help others achieve the necessary empowerment in order to do so. If you give Professor Devin a lemon, he would not only make lemonade but enterprise it!

Devin is a columnist, author and adjunct college professor of Economics, Business and Retail Management courses at several universities. For years he has been writing columns on the importance of business ownership and self-efficacy. Administrators, politicians, churches and other community leaders frequently request him for consulting or speaking.

Devin holds a Bachelor of Science Degree in Business Management and a Masters Degree in Business Administration. He is currently working on a Doctorate in Business Marketing. He resides in Atlanta, Georgia where he runs Going Against the Grain Group.

PREFACE:

This book is being written with the aspiring entrepreneur in mind. A large portion of the population is unhappy, as employees yet many possess the desire to become entrepreneurs. However, many new businesses tend to fail within the first two years. While it is true that some business fail due to bad locations, an overwhelming amount of new business fail simply because of the poor methods of management while running the operation.

There are many individuals who enter into the world of business simply because of desire. They feel that their expertise in a particular area validates them as being able to run their own business. This is a huge fallacy. Some fallacies like this. "Lisa knows how to cook so she would be able to run a successful restaurant." "Michael is a great mechanic, I bet he can open and grow a thriving mechanic shop." Some of us know these statements to be false, however we allow our emotions get the best of us and we embark on the quest of being an entrepreneur without being properly armed; sometimes resulting in the loss of thousands of dollars, broken marriages and financial destitution.

African-Americans are the race that has been through a significant uphill battle as citizens in the United States of America. African-Americans have been battling with social, economic and intellectual equality for the entire time we have been occupants of this country. This fight has made it even more difficult for us to be on one united front within our community.

The dysfunctions and mistrusts in our community are not coincidental nor entirely our fault. These mistrusts were mentally engraved in us through the calculated and strategic actions of individuals who oppressed blacks using the "Willie Lynch" theories. These theories included actions such as, "Bringing forth the strongest black male on the plantation to publicly beat and humiliate him in front of the other blacks. This action would cause the other blacks to mentally register that even the strongest black man was no match for the powerful white man or "slavery system."

Another calculated action was to, place the light-skinned slaves in the house to work and make them feel like they were better than the dark-skinned slaves. Then the slave-master would periodically have that light-skinned slave report to him the happenings of the other slaves, especially the secret plots of planning to escape. This classic action of "divide and conquer" would cause the slaves to always be fighting amongst themselves and therefore prohibited them from seeing the big picture of "in unity there is strength."

This book is not written to attack other races for running businesses that would otherwise be expected to be run by African-Americans. It is written to simply inform and empower (primarily) the aspiring African-American entrepreneur; though the teachings in the book can be applied in any community by any race. Many have the fortitude and determination but lack the fundamentals of running a business. Because this book is a step-by-step guide, failure is less likely to be imminent.

African-Americans do not create enough businesses in our communities leaving the opportunity for others. We need not be mad over the fact that other cultures have most of the businesses in our communities because the absence of their business possibly could have some neighborhoods in even worse shape. However, there are still opportunities.

Other cultures see the opportunity to become producers in our communities, while fill the roles of consumers within our own community. For years African-Americans have been faced with many challenges. Today we are facing an ever increasing challenge called the Black Beauty Supply industry. This industry's target market is African-Americans. African-Americans consume over 90% of the products in these beauty supply stores yet we own less than 5% of the stores. It is crucial that we understand the profound and negative effect this gross disparity is having on the African-American community.

Contrary to popular belief, there is no life without business. Many years ago, before the industrialization age, the Earth was filled with entrepreneurs with, if any, few employees. If an individual was unable to adopt a professional and business mindset, their quest for success may not be realized. An individual must be able to market and sell herself to employers before that individual is awarded a job. Likewise, individuals must properly balance their personal finances by assessing their income (gross sales), cash flow (operating income) and expenses (overhead) just to name a few. If someone can do this successfully, then opening a new business may not be farfetched.

There are two segments to an overall business structural function: the business operations and technical operations. Most people focus on the technical side. They tend to focus on being able to be a great chef and neglect marketing, customer service, market share, growth, payroll, taxes, etc. To be successful, the carpenter must know and understand business if she expects it to flourish. A detailed approach can be found in my new book, "Rebuilding the Black Infrastructure: Making America a Colorless Nation".

After reading this book, the average individuals with a desire for opening a lucrative beauty supply business will have a solid foundation to build from and succeed at it.

INTRODUCTION:

It's the summer of 2004 and my longtime friend approached me about going into business with him and opening a barber and beauty salon. At this point in my life, I was too busy releasing my first book, "The 180-Day Theory: Change through Empowerment", traveling and running my other businesses, to really give his proposition some serious consideration. He continued to speak to me about opening a salon and in the spring of 2005 we came to a formal agreement.

I was still busy traveling and had already begun writing my second book "Breaking the Cycle: Getting to Second Generational Prosperity" but I decided to take a break from my hectic schedule in order to ensure the business got off the ground properly. It took us several months but the establishment came out top-notch. I was proud of the salon and was dealing with the finishing touches. However, what I expected to be a short break from my writing wound up becoming the start of something much greater.

It was the summer of 2005. My cousin was visiting me from New York City. He wanted to see Atlanta and observe some of my business ventures. The hot topic was the salon. He was accompanying me around Atlanta while ran a few errands. I was in southwest Atlanta when I decided to stop into a beauty supply store to pick-up a few knick-knacks for my salon. Having these items on hand is convenient for the 12 stylists and prevents any disruptions in business due to a stylist having to run out and pick up certain items.

As we entered the store, we experienced the attempted intimidation that the storeowner tried to bestow on us. He was Asian. I have no problem with any race of people, however this day the Asian storeowner demonstrated that he had a problem with us African-Americans. He followed us throughout the store with a golf club for about 45 seconds, which felt like 45 minutes. I was not alarmed nor was my cousin. We concluded that this guy's perception of us was his problem because we both were stand-up and honest guys. Our maturity definitely paid off.

The Asian storeowner repeatedly asked me what was I looking for and my response remained the same, "Sir, I am just browsing for several items." His patience wore thin and he became belligerent. Then he yelled at me, "Get out now!" Although I was shocked and insulted, I decided to leave peacefully. As my cousin and I discussed what had just happened we grew angry and upset. We felt powerless which mad us angrier. My cousin caught a return flight to New York that same day. I headed back to my salon.

As I sat in the parking lot reflecting on how rude I was treated earlier at the Asian owned beauty supply store, I thought to myself, if this happened to me and I projected no type of suspicious appearance, he could be doing this to all of "us". I quickly came to the realization that I was not powerless. I could do my part to help put an end to this "poor treatment situation"...I can open a beauty supply store of my own. I am economically sound; I have business experience; I have a degree in business; and I have a staff of stylists that can aid and assist me in this process. With that thought, I jumped on the phone and called the owner of the building my salon was occupying and requested the suite next door to my salon. The owner stated that the suite had already been committed the day before and I could get another suite several doors down. I was persistent about my request and used my current salon business as leverage. I gave them until 5 o'clock to reply.

The office manager called me back an hour later and stated that they were able to let me occupy the suite next door. Prior to her call, I had begun interviewing my stylists getting them prepped for the undertaking because I believed I had God's favor and that the suite would be offered to me. Her call simply confirmed what I already knew.

This created an even greater delay in me getting back to working on my writing. I had to make opening the beauty supply store a priority, after all, I speak on self-development and taking control of one's life in the midst of oppression. I felt I had to set the example rather than accepting whatever was being handed to me. So in essence, I put my money where my mouth (well, pen) was.

My first store opened by the winter of 2005 and it was a whopping success. Was it easy? No. But I implemented many of the strong business practices that I developed over the years prior. I started my first store with no formal market research beyond me asking my friend, an African-American McDonald's owner sitting diagonal to my salon and future store. His response was direct. He stated, "Based on our research, an average of 15,000 motorists ride through our intersection daily." This confirmed my intuition and thus influenced my investment decision.

My first hurdle was finding out that some distributors required a minimum order of $5,000 while others required a minimum order of $10,000 before they would do business with me. Not to mention that there are no payment terms (credit) with distributors. (Well, at least for "us" there isn't. This is one of their "lookout for each other" tactics. Blacks typically don't have that type of cash at their disposal.)They expect to be paid upfront. I am not sure if this is their normal business practice, but from me that was what they required.

Many of the distributors are Korean. The intimidation at the retail stores was no match for that of the distribution building. Fortunately, I lived in South Korea for one year and was familiar with many of their customs and a few of their words. This experience gained me immediate access into their graces and they befriended me, on a business level of course. I remember thinking to myself how happy I was that I remained open minded when I resided in South Korea for that one year. Although I dreaded their cold weather, I was objective enough to try their foods, drinks and traditions. I even made a few Korean friends. Though these positive experiences lingered in my mind, the fact still remained that the distributor had to be paid upfront in order for me to get my items delivered. Remarkably, the distributor did not give me any attitude while taking my money.

To the glory of God and the support of loyal customers, I was able to open a second location after six months then a third location two months later. It wasn't until I became a part of this beauty supply industry that I learned of the vast disparity between black consumerism and black ownership. I learned of the different organizations that were created to help counteract this disparity. There is a DVD documentary that is being developed and constantly updated by filmmaker Aron Ranen. Get this. Aron is a Caucasian man. He is joining the movement of informing the black consumers of the disparity between the consumerism and ownership and why it exists.

As with any race, not all of the Asians are bad. In this industry you may find distributors, wholesalers and retailers of Asian descent that are quite friendly. Yet the black patrons that are the sole targeted consumers of these entrepreneurs are at their mercy. Should not blacks also have a stake in the ownership? However, since the Black race is seen to be a divided race for whatever the reason(s) may be, other races tend to enter the market of African-Americans and dominate the ownership of the businesses.

It is evident that some of our economic disparities lie beneath the problem of us being divided. To this day our stores get solicitors via telephone and walk-ins that first ask if we are Korean owned, when they learn we are not, they leave without presenting us with the opportunity to purchase their product(s) or service(s) they would have otherwise offered. There seems to be a code of solidarity among other races that we must develop and this book is a good start to getting the proper information out there for others who may have the desire but not the direction.

Part of the solution is to get aspiring business owners of these stores the right and necessary tools they need for success. Doing business can be the best experience a person can have but the person must have that strong business acumen to make it a great experience. I am going to discuss the solutions to many of the pitfalls African-Americans make while trying to do business. The problem in this industry is not that other races are dominating and doing business in it, the problem is... we are not!

CHAPTER 1
UNDERSTANDING THE INDUSTRY

HISTORY

A Culture Redefined

Hair care is defined as the overall care of the hair, from the root to the actual follicle. There are many different products that exist today to help the texture, growth and strengthening of the hair. Licensed professionals would often say, "The hair is as strong as your diet." Stress, trauma, medications and other activities of life plays a major role in how healthy the hair is. Next to one's nutrition, the actual care for the hair is important. Regular washing, conditioning and treating the hair is as important as the diet a person consumes.

Today, we have the commodity of coloring the hair, styling the hair and cutting the hair to whatever our liking is or to even keep up with any current trends. Products exist among us today that even counteract the loss of hair and the grain of hair. There are styling tools (equipment) that work together in unison with many of the chemical products available in the market today.

Up until the early 1900's, African-Americans were not given any tools or effective methods to treat their hair. As slaves, there was no true desire by the slave owners to help with the cosmetics of the blacks. Following the emancipation of slavery, slaves, like other races, had the desire to present themselves in an attractive context but lacked the convenient and effective means (items) to make it happen. There were simply no options available to the African-Americans to make their desires a reality.

This need is what helped to create the first self-made African-American female millionaire in this country, and some would even argue, in this world. Entrepreneurs always state, "You have to find a need and then fill it." This is what Madame CJ Walker did and did it oh so well.

Madame CJ Walker was born on Dec 23rd, 1867, just two years short of being born as a slave. She was born as Sarah Breedlove in Delta, Louisiana and spent her early years in the deep South where she worked picking cotton. When her parents died of yellow fever, she became an orphan at the age of seven, which some would say helped her hone her independence.

She married at the tender age of 14 and became a widow at the tender age of 20. She married two more times before her passing on May 25, 1919. However, before the passing of her short life, Walker ensured she passed a legacy for many generations to build from.

It has been said that the greatest victories often come from the greatest tragedies in one's life. Walker often turned her problems into opportunities. Walker became increasingly interested in hair care as a result of treating her own baldness caused by a scalp ailment. She worked temporarily as a tonic sales agent before founding her own company, the Madame C.J. Walker Manufacturing Company. Although she was not born a slave, she still worked like one. This work and courage eventually paid off. The Walker Company is where Walker invented and developed products to help soften the hair. Through the evolution of this product concept, we now refer to these products as relaxers and perms.

Her company was not only formed to develop products by securing patents, it was also developed to sell beauty care products and soon became a powerhouse company, being the largest African-American owned company in the United States in 1917. Walker soon employed many other African-Americans as sales agents, giving them career opportunities. Walker moved to St. Louis after the death of her first husband and toured the country with her third husband selling the beauty products. They moved the operation several times before settling in New York.

A generation apart from slavery, Walker was proud of her achievements, coming from being a cotton picker to an enterprising giant. She often participated in philanthropy work, leaving the majority of her personal wealth to charities. She was a regular speaker at NAACP rallies and conventions and pushed for the equality of black veterans. She became a tycoon by her desire to liberate many women from the strongholds of domestic work. Walker knew the intelligence of women was comparable to that of a man's despite their race or position. She became a positive influence for African-Americans of her time.

The thing about knowing the history in this or any other industry, community or country is it gives one the advantage to observe the direction of the current history and use it as a barometer to what was done in the past. It also gives insight as to what trends and strategies were already implemented and how successful the strategies were.

Fast-forward 40 years from her death and there became the birth of another trend, the hair weaves. African-American females are now interested in converting their hair to be more straight, curly, or bouncy without the use of chemicals. The weave also came in place as a quick fix to help women's immediate appearance that suffered from poor hair growth and treatment. It has now evolved to being more of a convenience for others. The weave was a solution of convenience for women who wouldn't or couldn't invest in the time it took for the products to produce results.

Hair care is just one vessel in the entire scope of beauty care. Beauty care consists of skin care, facial care, nail care and of course hair care. Understanding the history of hair care is not just informational and entertaining, it is also used to enlighten others of the path of the black beauty care industry. The history also helps give insight to the shifts in the trends and the shifts in the control of where and with whom it once began to where it is now heading and who is in control of it. Since the trend has shift so largely towards the demand for hair, the control began to slip away from the African-American grasp. We don't have intercontinental ties to countries that produce straight hair and this put us at a disadvantage.

In 1990 Congress passed an Act that allowed foreigners who invested one million dollars or more into the opening of a business and the business resulted in the hiring of 10 or more employees immediate citizenship. This is another evidence of evolution of the country where African-Americans tend to lose any control we once had due to the lack of strong economics. Typically, when an African-American produces something that is cutting-edge, in order for the industry or empire to stay in the control of African-Americans, the economical power must also be strong. Media Mogul Bob Johnson, the founder of B.E.T., was not able to keep the ownership of B.E.T. in the hands of Blacks largely due to our collective lack of wealth as an ethnic group.

Running large empires and keeping the control of it starts with knowing how to run and manage small businesses. If we can understand the concept of running a neighborhood retail store then we can absolutely get to the point where we can operate

6

distribution points and this is where the solution to our inability to get back into the ownership of this industry will begin to be solved. This book is just the start. YOU are the finish!

OUR DIFFICULTIES

Of course there are issues within the African-American community that has helped to enable the loss of an industry we were expected to control. Difficulties stretch further than what we are outwardly faced with. As Willie Lynch's concept goes, "If we create a divide within the black community, this will help to perpetuate slavery." This outlook has become a popular conceptual adage that many of us fail to identify or fail to attempt to correct. There is no doubt that African-Americans have experienced severe hardship in this country that has added to the dissolution of our unity. However, the more we disband as a people the more and easier we allow ourselves to be exploited. The simple solution is for black consumers to form a united front. This united front starts with individuals and can eventually spread throughout the entire community and race. This lack of unity spirals into other areas of functions in our community.

Here is an excerpt from U.S. President Barack Obama's book "Dreams from My Father" as he was trying to form a movement within a Chicago suburban community in his younger years. You will be able to see that this problem within our community is not isolated. It exists from the Atlantic Ocean to the tips of the Pacific Ocean:

> "That's the real deal, right here," Rafiq said. "People from outside our community making money off us and our brothers and sisters disrespect. Basically what you got here is Koreans and Arabs running the stores, the Jews still owning most of the buildings. Now in the short term, we're here to make sure that the interests of black people are looked after, you understand. When we hear one of them Koreans is mistreating a customer, we gonna be on the case. We gonna insist that they respect us and make a contribution back to the community – fund our programs, what have you...

"You won't hear me complaining about the Koreans," he said, stacking a few more boxes by the door. "They are the only ones that pay their dues into the Chamber [of Commerce]. They understand business, what it means to cooperate. They pool their money. Make each other loans. We don't do that, see. The black merchants around here, we're all like crabs in a bucket..."

Words spoken by non-fictional characters in "Dreams of My Father (1995). Obama Barack, Three Rivers Press.

DISTRIBUTION CHANNEL

There are several points in the channel of distribution. They are: Manufacturer, Distributor, Retailer and Consumer. Once we are divided as a person, we become divided as consumers. Once we become divided as consumers, it makes it difficult for us to climb into the ownership saddle. There is still a diverse group of manufacturers but distribution is where the shift in diversity begins and transcends to the other points in the distribution channel. Distributors are the business within the channel that gets the various products to the retail stores.

These distributors carry a large range of products and have a lot of control over the retail business. They decide whom they will do business with and how business will be conducted. There are rules within some of these distributors that implement a mileage radius strategy. Meaning, if your store is too close to another one of their stores, they will refuse to do business with you. Then there are the payment policies. Although distributors have the ability to check your business' credit history, time in business, and other factors to determine whether or not they will do business with you, they rarely do. They will often demand cash payment upfront before they would release any product putting an additional strain on the retail owner.

Meanwhile, there are some stores that open solely on credit terms with some distributors for whatever reason, giving them a greater competitive edge over other businesses in the market. Having a distributor in the channel makes it very easy for the manufacturers. Without the distributors, the manufacturers would be forced to deal with thousands of stores in order to get their products to the consumers. Distributors take the burden off of the manufacturers and act as a "one-stop" shop for the retailers. In order to become a distributor, it often requires a large capital investment ranging in the millions of dollars. Typically, African-Americans are not financially equipped to become retailers let alone distributors.

Working together could allow African-Americans the ability to hurdle this obstacle. This is where a divisive ideology hinders the ability to become controllers of this industry. Until we are able to become owners of that "crucial" point in the distribution channel all hopes are lost. Learning to run a retail operation will get us the needed experience to be able to successfully create, manage and fulfill thousands of retail stores when we become distributors.

Consumers

Focusing on ourselves causes us to only pay attention to what is beneficial to us, as individuals, and not us as a whole. Consumers go into facilities and focus on two things, price and variety. Since we do not control distribution and it is extremely difficult for us to get into the retail business, obstacles cause the African-American owners to make decisions that are sometimes not favorable to the customer. Prices may not be as attractive to the customer and this not because of a deliberate decision by the owner, it is often because of the "cash and carry" policy that is imposed on the owner giving them less leeway on their cash cycle for the store.

Other stores sometimes get preferential treatment, such as the terms described earlier. When the customer sees a smaller inventory or less variety, they would typically criticize the business and head over to another store most times not owned by an African-American. In other communities, another race cannot easily set-up a business and it thrive regardless of the price of the items. Focusing more on the big picture within the community makes for a better solution. This big picture not only applies to the beauty supply industry, one that we should be in great control of, but it applies to all others.

Hair

The hair is a very important product in the livelihood of a beauty supply store. The sad part to this is hair usually comes from the Asian continent, which gives Asians a greater advantage of distributing the hair. This is an obstacle that is very difficult to circumvent. The only way totally around it is for the women to practice abstinence of it and eliminate the need for it in the marketplace or for us to develop black owned hair distribution companies that import the hair directly from the continent of Asia (most commonly China).

Start-Up

Obtaining the needed capital to start any business is a massive problem among African-Americans. The lack of being able to obtain the capital is more so a symptom than the problem. African-Americans contribute billions to the consumer spending that is reported annually. Shifting what money is being spent on is the focus that must be adjusted. Although we are becoming more financially astute and economically conscious, there still lies a huge disparity in the amount of *wealth* blacks are able to accumulate as opposed to other races.

Wealth is accumulated to add to the strength of a person's financial soundness. Huge incomes do not necessarily lead to wealth. African-Americans have managed to become competitive in the marketplace and increase their level of earned income. Yet, there is still a tremendous need for conscious awareness in spending, saving and investing. I was once told, "We lose more money in missed opportunities than the money we are able to make from the opportunities we are able to capitalize on." I am sure opportunities come along where you wished you held the capital in order to be able to seize the opportunity but was unable to. If we live with the possibility of opportunities coming our way, we will be placing ourselves in *wealthy* positions and if those opportunities never do come along, well hey, what's the worse that could happen? We live financially free because we continued to accumulate wealth anyway.

News Flash...In writing this book I am presenting you the opportunity to get into an industry that can reap extrinsic and intrinsic, measurable and immeasurable, and financial and non-financial rewards!

Understanding Retail

Operating a retail store goes beyond simply hoping a customer walks through your door. Billions of money in the retail industry is made outside of "hopes". Money is made by being deliberate, not wishful. With the increase in competition and fickle customer demand, retailers must have a much clearer understanding of the supply chain in its entirety. There are several stops in the supply chain before getting the product to the customer. These stops each have unique objectives and different requirements. There is the manufacturer, distributor (supplier, wholesaler), retailer and consumer. Below is a diagram that illustrates this description.

Manufacturer	Distributor Supplier	Retailer (YOU)	Consumer ($$$)

Then, you must consider Sales and Marketing, Retail Operations Management, Administration, Inventory, Taxes, Expenditures, Loss Management and Human Resources (Payroll, Training, Research and Development). Despite all of these considerations, running a *retail operation* can be very rewarding! It really isn't too difficult, especially if you start off on the right foot. The lack of reward to the owner/manager/entrepreneur is when they do not have a good clear understanding of how retail really works. Even the smallest retail operations are faced with the same challenges as the Big-Box Retailers such as, Target and Wal-Mart. The issues are the same, only the dollars at risk may be different. However, smaller retailers can relish in knowing they have a better profit margin and simpler operations, making them the heartbeat of the local economy. Risking savings and other personal assets is a hard pill to swallow for many aspiring retail owners and this is why we serve the purpose we do. We help you avoid all of the costly and common mistakes made by inexperienced and seasoned store owners. If you really understand retail, then you should understand that our university **MUST** be your first stop! Ensure you get enrolled if you haven't done so already…

CHAPTER 2
PLANNING

Planning (Chapter 2)

The Business Plan

Planning is a very important practice in our everyday lives. Without it, we would most likely live in disarray. We must plan when we are going to make appointments, when we are going to take vacation and when we are going to make life-altering decisions. If we simply acted on a whim, the results may not be favorable. This is the same concept in the world of business. Before a person embarks on entrepreneurship, especially when that individual is quitting a job to do so, the plan must be comprehensive, realistic and robust. The first suggestion to give an individual is to develop a business plan and an operational plan. This is imperative if you do not have any business experience or managerial experience.

From the outside looking in, a business can seem like a simple undertaking, but when you take the role of accountant, sales manager, operations manager, marketing director, procurement specialist, inventory manager, comptroller, shipping and receiving and other roles it can become overwhelming. Knowing what to do "in the event of" is important.

There is no right recommendation for developing a business plan. Some people may seek the help of an outside source to help them construct it, which is fine once you know the contents of the business plan. Don't shy away from the tedious aspects of the business, such as planning, in the beginning. Since you will need to possess the ability to function in all capacities, it is important for you to know and understand them. Later in this book, we will go into detail about some of the components of a business plan. In this chapter, we will simply outline the basic components of the business plan. This is a format of a business plan you can find in any in business book, the library or on the Internet:

For further assistance log onto
www.beautysupplyinstitute.com

Mission Statement
- ♦ A clear statement of your company's overall mission (Use words that will help direct the growth of your company, but be as concise as possible)

The Team
- ♦ List CEO and key management by name
- ♦ Include previous accomplishments to show these are people with a record of success
- ♦ Summarize number of years of experience in this field

Market Summary
- ♦ Market: past, present, & future:
  - — Review those changes in market share, leadership, players, market shifts, costs, pricing, or competition that provide the opportunity for your company's success

Opportunities
- ♦ Problems and opportunities:
  - — State consumer problems, and define nature of product/service opportunities created by those problems

Business Concept
- ♦ Summarize key technology, concept or strategy on which your business is based

Competition
- ♦ Summarize competition
- ♦ Outline your company's competitive advantage

Goals & Objectives
- ♦ Five-year goals
  - — State specific measurable objectives
  - — State market share objectives
  - — State revenue/profitability objectives

Financial Plan
  ◆   High-level financial plan that defines financial model, pricing assumptions, and reviews yearly expected sales and profits for the next three years
  ◆   Use several slides to cover this material appropriately

Resource Requirements
  ◆   Technology requirements
  ◆   Personnel requirements
  ◆   Resource requirements

  —Financial, distribution, promotion, etc.

  —External requirements

  —Products/services/technology required to be purchased outside company

Cost Benefit/Analysis
This includes laying out the cost of your business versus the benefits that business will produce. For example, will the cost of your business be far less than the actual benefit it will bring to you.

Risks & Rewards
Risks

  —Summarize risks of proposed project
Addressing risk

  —Summarize how risks will be addressed

Rewards

  —Estimate expected pay-off, particularly if seeking funding

Key Issues
Near term

  —Isolate key decisions and issues that need immediate or near-term resolution
Long term

  —Isolate issues needing long-term resolution

  —State consequences of decision postponement

If you are seeking funding, state specifics

Budgeting

Part of your business plan is to establish a budget. This budget will give you an idea of how much of a store you would like to open. Based on your investment capital, determine how much you can pay per square footage, how much revenue would be needed to satisfy your fixed costs and variable costs. We will go into detail later in the book on how to determine all of these aspects of the business.

The Operations Plan

The Operations Plan is very similar to that of a business plan as far as outlying the plan but is different in its concept. An operations plan is much like a strategic plan in which it guides the employees of the business in what direction they should go "in the event of". The operations plan focuses on the functions of each department. Bare in mind, the company can possess multiple operations plan for each business function. The operations plan should have a simple overview of these areas, Goal Prioritizing, Operations Efficiency, Improvement and Growth Strategies and Resource Identification and Allocation.

Performing the S.W.O.T.T. Analysis

Before determining to take any direction within the company, you may first want to perform an S.W.O.T.T. analysis. S.W.O.T.T. stands for Strengths, Weaknesses, Opportunities, Threats and Trends. This analysis is helpful in identifying whether a particular move within the business or a move for the overall business is a wise idea.

Strengths

What are the points in this decision that will make the move lucrative or a success? You will want to take an inventory of any skills, talents or resources that are available that will help the choice to be a beneficial one. Strength in deciding whether to open the beauty supply business can simply be there is a market for it. While another strength could be, you have experience with the products. The strengths are not limited to one or two things. The list can go on and on. Applying the

S.W.O.T.T. in many of the critical decisions can give you a clearer vision to whether or not the decision is well thought out.

Weaknesses

Some people look at weaknesses as a bad thing, but weaknesses can turn themselves into opportunities. Most people hate to think that weaknesses exist but they do. Others are intimidated by weaknesses but you shouldn't be. A weakness can easily be turned into strengths with enough hard work. Weaknesses could be not having enough financial resources to expand, no experience in retail, or fear. This fear could cause a business owner to quickly retreat back to the world of Corporate America with the slightest sign of trouble. In my second book, *Breaking the Cycle: Getting to Second Generational Prosperity,* I explained how to properly navigate through the fear syndrome. Weaknesses are there to identify what areas we can improve in. We are human, so there will be weaknesses.

Opportunities

Opportunities are being able to capitalize on a current situation. There may be an opportunity existing in the market that other businesses are not able to build on or have failed to identify. Maybe you have a specific niche that you will be offering or a partnership you plan to setup between your business and another business. Then there are opportunities that may only be available to you, such as intrinsic opportunities. Intrinsic opportunities can come in the form of being able to model entrepreneurship behavior to your children, manage your own destiny, to help family members gain employment or simply have total control of your future. Opportunities also help to paint the picture of whether or not a decision should be made.

Threats

Threats are similar to weaknesses. Threats are indications in the market or personally that can stifle the potential growth of the business. Threats can be present competition, market crime or weather. A threat is anything that can be threatening to the business.

Trends

Trends are just that, trends. Perhaps the market is going from shopping in stores to shopping online. There are trends that help businesses grow and help others meet its demise if it doesn't innovate itself or stay ahead of the trend curve. Stockpiling on products that may be trendy can leave a business with a stagnant inventory. Entertainers constantly create trends within the marketplace that consumers grab a hold to. Once the entertainers' song or movie looses its buzz, the trend will be gone. It is also important to the decision process to understand if the business idea is perceived as a trend.

Product Life Cycle

There are four stages to the Product Life Cycle: Introduction, Growth, Maturity and Decline. The Product Life Cycle is determining the stages of a product.

♦ Introduction - When a product becomes available to the market, it is in its Introduction Stage. The Introduction Stage is where the product is heavily marketed and often makes the bulk of its money.

♦ Growth - The Growth Stage is where the product begins to secure a growing portion of the market share.

♦ Maturity - The Maturity Stage is when the product has reached its peak and is no longer a desirable product to the consumers in the marketplace.

♦ Decline - The Decline Stage is the stage where the product begins to lose its market share. This often happens when there are new trends in the marketplace or the product is now being replaced by another product.

The Product Life Cycle is a theory you can apply to the market. You can look at it as the Market Life Cycle. Determine what stage the market is currently in: Introduction, Growth, Maturity or Decline. This strategy will help you also determine where you would like your store to be, which we will be discussing next.

CHAPTER 3
DETERMINING YOUR MARKET SELECTION

Determining Your Market Selection (Chapter 3)

Determining where you would like your store to be is probably the most important decision you will make. Once this decision is made, you have to stick with it during the duration of your stay. In this decision, you will also want to do an S.W.O.T.T. analysis. During this S.W.O.T.T. analysis you want to also incorporate the Market Product Life Cycle. When you are shopping for locations, property managers tend to not disclose the downside to their locations. If they do, they will ensure they give you 20 upsides per one downside. It is important for you to do your own research before agreeing to anything with the property manager. Most times, their lease will be firm and present little leeway in you being able to get out of it. So ensure you are happy with your location decision.

What to look for?

It has been said that location is everything. It's not EVERYTHING but just about. Your location must have a presentable appeal and be highly visible. As I stated in the introduction, I got information on how much the traffic flow was in the area for my first location. In business it is not realistic to assume you will capture 100% of the market and retain 100% of your customers. Your retention base will be as high as your customer service and product fulfillment. You want to select a location that is large enough to house the products you want but small enough to make the store feel stocked.

If your initial investment is small, the store may appear as if it is not properly stocked even though you may have purchased thousands of dollars worth of inventory. The customers want to feel secure while shopping at your store. If they feel like you are not going to last, they may be skeptical about shopping with you. If you plan on reinvesting the revenues generated in the first few months in order to grow the inventory to the store's capacity, ensure the customers knows this by restricting an area for them to shop or by constructing a temporary drywall so they will believe this is the total size of the store. As time and sales progress you can expand the wall to suit.

When determining your market, you want to study your targeted clients. You will want to visit the area (if you are not aware of it) several times for lengthy periods before committing to any location. Study the foot traffic flow (pedestrians) and determine how well you are able to see your proposed location as oncoming traffic. If you are already dead set on what products you would like to specialize in, then observe the market based on those products. If you are open to what type of products you would like to offer, then attempt to establish what specialty would fit best.

Let's discuss the specializing of products. In the beauty supply industry, there are many different types of products that go with the different types of persons. You may have a high client base for individuals that are interested in natural hair products, such as products for dreadlocks or non-processed hair. People that favor these products would like the products to compliment what they would like their hair to look like. If this is the case, then you will also need to carry accessories that would go with these individuals wardrobe. Without actually stereotyping, for the most part, these persons would also like natural art jewelry, natural scarves and natural looking bandannas for their wearing.

Then you may have a large population of individuals that have damaged hair. This can be for a number of reasons. It could be a high trendy area that has processed and styled their hair into damage. It could be a low-income area where the customers are unable to get quality hair care service consistently. It could also be an area where the toxins in the air have caused damage to the hair. It could be an area where most of the customers work in a plant or quarry and is unable to keep their hair protected properly due to work conditions. It could also be the diet of the person in that area. There are many different reasons for hair damage and if you want to specialize in the treatment of it, like some hair stylists, then you may want to see if there is a population that could sustain your business.

You may have a market that is very trendy and requires the latest products on the market. As you will see, when a manufacturer is highly marketing their product, there will be a high request rate for their product. If the market is constantly being saturated with the *latest and greatest* advertising then be prepared to be able to fill these requests.

4. Your market may be a seasoned market that has been around for a while or is populated by an older age range of individuals. If this is the case, you will want to invest in products that have been around for a long time. People that have been using a product for a long time tend to stick with it. They have been loyal to this product for quite some time and will not easily change to another product. Be aware of this fact and know what market you are attempting to enter.

5. If you would like to start a beauty supply retail store and are flexible on what products you will offer, then you can decide simply by the need of the market. If you already know what line of products you would like to offer or specialize in, then your search will be to seek out your target market and then you would have to determine the need in that market once those target customers are found. Determining your market based on the specialty is something to always consider, simply having a saturation of people is not enough to go on.

When you have identified that a market exists for your store, then you have to take your research one step further. To determine if your location may be successful, you will want to identify the number of customers that reside or populate the market in a 3-mile radius. For a loosely populated market, you may extend the radius to 5 or 7 seven miles. Once you have determined your fixed costs, then you will need to establish how much your flat daily revenue would need to be to survive. If your total fixed cost is $4,500 per month then if you open 6 days per week, you will need to generate $187.50 per day in order to satisfy the fixed expenses. Then you will want to determine how many sales you would need to make and at what rate. For example, if you average $12 per sale then you would need to make 16 sales per day in order to meet your daily fixed expenses. How will you know your average? It's hard to determine your average before the store opens but you should open your doors with whatever figure you've determined in mind and make the sales with being able to acquire a minimum it. In this case, that would be $12 per sale. The average revenue per sale will be tied to the class level of your market. This is where obtaining the demographics is important. The demographics report will outline the number of individuals in the market that you are targeting and their median income. It's different in varying markets.

GOOD !

When you have established the number of sales you need to see per day, identify if you can sustain this number realistically based on the target market density, or number of the people in the market that will fit the mold of a potential shoppers. For starters your base daily number of sales (needed sales) should be no less than 1% of the target market. So if we use the existing number of sales we have been using in this case, 16, then your target market's presence should be in the range of 38,400. How did I get this number? 16 sales per day at 24 days in the month (based on a 6-day work week) totals 384 sales per month. At this formula you would see that 384 equals to 1% of 38,400. You would want to have a minimum sales count of 384 per month at an average of $16 with a total of $4500 in fixed expenses.

After this is obtained, you will want to set a realistic goal as time progresses. Ultimately, you will want to secure a minimum of 10% of the target population on a monthly basis. This number is 3,840 sales. Multiply this number by an average ticket sale of $12 per month and you could be on your way to seeing substantial monetary rewards. Securing this goal is not an easy feat but it can be done. Continue reading.

Within the radius you establish, identify your competition and if you will be able to compete. If the competition has been there for a while, it may be a little difficult to draw customers to your location. It's not impossible however especially if you identify a niche that the competition is not employing and heavily drive it.

This stage is just your preliminary. You will not want to select a market as of yet. Selecting the market comes at a later step in the process and it comes at a later time in the process for a reason. At this point, you should only be researching the market and assessing the possibilities.

CHAPTER 4
ESTABLISHING
YOUR NICHE

Establishing Your Niche (Chapter 4)

How do I establish my niche? Your niche will be what will make your business appealing to draw customers. This niche will also have to be something that you plan to continuously focus on because you will want this niche to be one of the reasons the customers decide to do business with you. There are several niche opportunities to consider in the beauty supply retail industry. They are service,[1] convenience,[2] pricing,[3] appeal,[4] specials,[5] and cross-functions.[6] These are not all the niches that exist. You can also apply the strategies that will be discussed on these niches to whichever niche you decide to pursue.

Service

Service is one of the first things a customer picks up on. Some time or another we've all been customers that have experienced good and bad customer service. This service comes in many forms. Employees offer us service and the business does as well. Waiting on a shopping buggy, an item not being priced or having to wait for a manager's override are all forms of customer service. Some businesses may be expensive to shop at, however there service may be so phenomenal that the customers decide to continue doing business with them because they know they will receive the best service.

Convenience

Convenience can also be placed into the *service* category but convenience also plays a larger role. There may be a much larger beauty supply store in your market radius yet there can still be market share opportunities in that same market. Larger stores tend to be much more difficult to navigate through when time is of the essence. Parking your vehicle is often a time staking experience, and then getting in and out of the store can also eat up much of your time. Going back to service, when there is an incompetent staff, this can also cause additional inconvenience for the customer. Do not feel threatened by the competition. Often time they are not capitalizing on all of the niches that exist in that market.

Having convenient store hours is another niche. There are stores that open 24 hours and 7 days per week. This gives the customer full control of when they can visit the location. This is something that can be considered but you must also be careful not to open a can of worms that you cannot control. The operation of a 24-hour location is a sizeable undertaking and must be approached with caution. Simply opening early and closing late is a niche that can give customers enough reason to shop with you. Some stores also open 7 days per week. Finding your niche in the convenience of store hours is something to consider. There are some storeowners that have poor operating hours because they run the business as an owner/operator yet they are successful. They are most likely providing other niches that wash away the plague of poor operating hours. These owners may have a niche such as being former hair stylists that has a clientele and are very knowledgeable with the products.

Reliability also goes with the niche of convenience. When a customer knows she can come to your location and get exactly what she needs and is confident the item will be in stock, she will more than likely become a faithful customer. A customer that has no vehicle and must rely on public transportation does not have the option of "shopping around". When they get off of that bus, they must be confident that your store has what they need. When a stylist has someone under the dryer at their salon and they decide to run out to your location, they want to know that you have what they are looking for. Satisfying the customer through reliability is an intrinsic value that truly cannot be measured.

Pricing

When determining your price points, you will want to be realistic yet strategic in your approach. Your demographic research and market comparison will be able to help you determine where to set your prices. However, depending on your niche, your prices can vary quite a bit from the competition.

There are three types of pricing strategies: they are Profit Pricing, Sales Pricing and Status Quo Pricing. Let's start with Profit Pricing. Profit Pricing simply means setting your prices to get the largest profit per sale. This strategy is seen as the higher end of the pricing scale. The upside to this strategy is the profit margin per sale is higher and with right customer volume, can provide a lucrative cash flow. The downside to this strategy is it tends to lower the customer count.

2

Sales Pricing is when pricing is on the lower end of the spectrum. Sales Pricing occurs when the owner or manager is not too concerned about the profit margin as much as they are with the customer count. The upside to this, of course, is the store will attract a higher number of customers. The downside to this is your profit margin will be lower causing you have to generate more customers to meet your revenue goals. This tends to be a practice when a new store opens. Sales Pricing along with specials and coupons are typically available in the early days of the store's opening. Large companies and franchises usually do not have to implement this strategy since their prices are well established.

3.

Status Quo Pricing means to price with the competition or the market. This happens when the competition is well established in the market and a lower profit margin is not desired. Many stores come into the market and implement Status Quo Pricing in order to not rock the boat with the consumers.

If you would like to utilize pricing as your store's niche, you will have to first consider these different options. Determine whether or not there is an existing opportunity for niche pricing. Even if there isn't, there could be a possibility for you to create one. Deciding on which price structure you choose to utilize is for you to determine.

4 *Appeal*

Appeal is a niche that many retail stores capitalize on. The appeal niche can be placed into your secondary niche. However, there are businesses that sell the concept to appeal well. In an industry where the consumers make up 90% of the sales, appeal may not be a bad niche to consider. When I say appeal, I refer to the attractiveness of the store. How clean the store is. How well the products are laid out. How up to date are the fixtures. In these days, when customers walk into a store that has a nice appeal, they issue a compliment. Compliments are only issued when there is something that presents itself above expectations. When a person gets a compliment for an outfit or for their performance, it simply means that it exceeds what was typically expected. In this case, beauty supply stores have developed the reputation of not being well organized. For whatever reason this may be, there is definitely a niche of appeal that can be created, turning this reputation problem into an opportunity to gain customers through this niche.

Specials

Offering specials is something that many companies use to drum up business. Often times, they use specials when business is slow. This is not a bad thing. To maximize the store's profit margin, you may want to not offer specials since offering specials can decrease your profit margin unless you utilize the "leading loss" concept. The leading loss concept is where a business will offer a product at a very low price and sometimes at even a loss, in order to cross-sell (to be discussed) another product that will make the entire package a profitable sale. You can implement a regular amount of sales of products or to individuals such as, licensed stylists, cosmetology instructors or cosmetology students. These specials can become a regular routine at your location giving your business a niche to maximize.

Cross-Functions

Cross-function of a business occurs when a company offers a similar product or service in addition to what their primary function is. For example, a barbershop may have a nail technician in their shop that handles nail services while the female's husband, boyfriend or child is being serviced. This cross-function capability can exist in beauty supply as well.

You may be able to offer, delivery services, body piercing, styling, and braiding and in some cases, professional products. These services can help your store become closer to being a one-stop shopping experience. The world's largest retail chain, Wal-Mart, practices this niche. In addition to offering some of the lowest prices in the marketplace, they offer salon services, tax services and eye care services.

Before you begin practicing the cross-functionality technique in your store, I strongly recommend you research if what you are trying to do is allowed in your location or if it is within code to offer that service. Salons require certain specifications within its location in order to begin servicing clients. Manufacturers of some professional products do not allow their products to be sold in retail stores. They are to only be sold in salons. Lastly, if you plan on being located in a mall or strip plaza and there is a salon in that building, that salon may have exclusivity in offering salon services. If you invest in housing a salon within your store without doing research and this is the case, your investment may be a total loss to you being that you won't be able to operate that function within your store.

Specialty

The final niche to be discussed is the specialty. Once you have determined your market and who your target customers are, you should have an idea of what you can specialize in. If your store will be based around the natural hair care and those customers then providing a niche in the area should be to target those customers as well. Here are some options for you to choose from based on who your target market is:

- Natural Hair Services & Products
- Damaged Hair
- New Products
- Traditional Products

With this list you can determine your niche. Some customers search high and low for products that they have been using for 30 years. When they discover that you sell this "traditional product" you will probably have gained a customer for life. Developing a niche of specialized products is something that can be explored and provide a lucrative direction for the business.

CHAPTER 5

BECOMING A LEGAL ENTITY

Becoming a Legal Entity (Chapter 5)

Selecting a business type

Opening a beauty supply store requires commitment. If you are unable to commit yourself to a business whole-heartedly, then this may not be the business for you. This commitment is an entirely separate world from your personal world. It should not be treated as a home-based business or a multi-level marketing business. The general public will view this business respectfully. The amount of respect the consumer awards to you is strictly up to you.

You should not attempt to run this business under the legal radar. What I mean by this is, do not try to avoid reporting to Uncle Sam in any way shape or form. This can definitely come back to haunt you, especially when your business becomes a whopping success. You will want to build your business with a very solid foundation. You will want to have your business in compliance. When the business goes into operation, these are not things that you will want to revert back to take care of later.

Before getting started, you will need to determine what form of business structure you will operate under. There are five different types. There are sole-proprietorship, partnership, Limited Liability Company, corporation and non-profit organization.

When a business operates as a sole-proprietorship, the owner and the business united as one entity. This means if something was to go wrong with the business such as the business being held liable for an accident, owing money on business debt or tax reporting, the owner would also be personally held liable. This is typically not the best structure for any business that is making large contact with the general public.

Partnership is when two or more parties or persons come together and jointly own the business. There are several different types of partnerships. How the partnership is constructed is up to the parties involved. One party (business) or person may have more ownership than the other and one party can also be known as a silent partner whereas they simply collect on the earnings but has no operational input; this is called a Limited Partnership. Then you have Limited Liability Partnership and General Partnership. You can get the full details of each partnership structure at your local library.

3   Limited Liability Company is very unique as it offers the same legal protection as that of a corporation but has less tax requirements. An LLC can consist of one or more managers. Its structure allows members of the organization to contribute to the management of the organization. Because of its low-cost annual registration dues and tax breaks, LLC is a becoming a very popular business setup for new small businesses.

4.   There are several different types of corporations. If you plan on employing a large number of individuals, 100 or more, this may be a good option for you. It has been said that a corporation poses the least amount of personal liability in the business world, however the taxes are typically more. You can be exposed to double taxation depending on your corporation type.

5.   Non-profit organizations are organizations that exist for the betterment of the community and not the betterment of its owners. Non-profit organizations generate revenue from membership dues, donations, grants and more. But they are not allowed to generate revenue from sales. This would mean that your revenue would not be allowed to come from product sales.

I suggest you consult an attorney and tax professional before deciding which route you would like to pursue before becoming a legal entity.

Selecting a name

Think carefully on the name you would like to use. Remember, you are trying to appeal to a large and diverse audience. Though you may be trying to attract African-American customers, not all African-Americans think alike. There are different religions, traditions and cultures that exist within this community and stereotyping the likes and dislikes can be a grave mistake. Ensure that the name you select can appeal to all age ranges and backgrounds. Once the name is selected run a name search through your local Secretary of State's database to ensure the name is available. If it is, reserve it immediately. There may be a $25 cost but, it will be well worth it. The name may be available when you search it and after you begin registrations, it may be taken. So the $25 acts as your insurance policy in being awarded the name you chose and reserved. The name reservation usually reserves the name for 90 days; however check with your state's requirements.

Some people move forward without registering their names figuring they can go back and take care of it but your business name may become so attractive that someone else may decide to use it across town and if you are not properly registered, they can easily send you, the originator of the name, a "cease and desist" letter forcing you to halt the usage of that name. This concept is the same as having logos unregistered. You will want to visit www.uspto.gov to secure the legal use of your logos.

Coming into existence

1. Once you determine how you will setup the business, you will need to obtain a Federal Employer Identification Number also known as an FEIN or Tax Id number. This number takes only a few moments to obtain by phone at 1-800-829-4933 or on-line by visiting www.irs.gov. When obtaining your FEIN, you will have to issue the IRS (Internal Revenue Service) a name for your business. You can get this number without having a concrete business address and submit an address change with this agency.

2. Next, you will need to register your business with the state. Whatever business structure you decide to go with, you will need to submit the registration documents with your Secretary of State's office. You can contact them to obtain the documents. Most of the time, you can find their agency through a search on the Internet and typically, the documents will be available.

3. The next thing you will need to do is obtain a sales tax ID number. You can get this through your state's Department of Revenue office. This tax ID number, also known as the State Tax ID gives you the right to resell products as a retailer. Without this, you cannot collect sales tax and will not be in compliance with the government if you are retailing products.

IMPORTANT

At this point you may be wondering why you are obtaining all these legal documents before you even have a location. This is because the distributors will not even converse with you if you do not exist legally and your very next step will be to identify your suppliers.

Identifying Suppliers

Identifying suppliers will be a tricky step in the process. There are many suppliers (distributors) throughout the country, but deciding which supplier you will want to do business with is a major decision. You will want to practice the Japanese originated "Just-In Time Inventory". This method will be discussed later. For right now, you will want to identify a supplier that is reputable and located geographically attractive to your proposed location. You will also want to develop your budget. Your budget cannot be determined unless you get the prices of the products from the suppliers. So as you can see, in this phase of the process you will be looking for a few needs that the supplier can fulfill: price, location and reliability. Some suppliers will not do business with you if you are located in an area close to a competitor they already do business with. They will go by the address on your forms to determine where you are located. So this is more tricky and risky than it may seem. Let's recap. In order to obtain quotes, you need licenses. In order to obtain licenses, you need an address. In order to obtain an address, you need a lease.

Let's think logically. Now suppose I sign a lease and the market is unavailable for that distributor? This is why determining who your suppliers will be ahead of time is very important. It is much easier to determine if the market is a new one and there are no current stores doing business in it. Navigating your way through this phase is not easy. You will have to use creative strategizing in order to get through this part. The bright side of this is, some distributors will allow you to inquire with them a proposed address and they respond whether or not the address is available for you to do business with them. To get you started, here are two chemical distributors, one hair distributor and two manufacturers that are fairly easy to deal with. None of these listed are Korean owned.

Preferred Contact List of Beauty Supply Distributors

(More Distributors and a Complete Listing of Manufacturers can be found in the *Beauty System Resource Book* found at www.beautysupplysystem.com)

Distributors
Carib Sales, Inc.
4500 N.W. 135 St.
Opa - Locka (Miami) Florida 33054
Phone: 305-688-5731
Toll Free: (888) 84Carib / (888) 842-2742
Fax: 305-681-5683
www.caribsalesinc.com

TWT Distributing, Inc.
11107-C South Commerce Blvd.
Charlotte, NC 28273
Phone: 704-588-1746
Toll Free: 800-849-7898
Sales Rep/Mr. Ike Rudd: 609-472-6628
Fax: 704-587-0489
www.twtdist.com

Hair Manufacturer
Jaguar Luxury Remi Hair
Showroom location
4235 Lancaster Avenue
Philadelphia, Pa. 19104.
Phone: 215-382-1523
Fax: 215-382-1524.

Main office
Phone: 215-472-7216
Fax: 215-472-7218
www.ctwhairboutique.com

Manufacturers
Fabric Naturals
2219 W. Olive Ave. #300
Burbank, CA 91506
Toll Free: 877-942-6322 ext 86
Fax: 877-942-6322
www.FabricNaturals.com

Kizure Products
1950 North Central Avenue
Compton, CA 90222
Phone: 310-604-0021
Fax: 310-604-0334
www.kizureironworks.com

CHAPTER 6
BUDGETING

Budgeting (Chapter 6)

Building Out

Opening a brand new location has its pros and cons.
Some pros are:

1.   You will be the first to introduce the industry to the market. (HUGE PRO!)
2.   You have the opportunity to seize a significant market share. (HUGE PRO!)
3.   You can set a standard of operation so high that it will be difficult for competitors to enter and compete.
4.   You can become a monopoly.
5.   You can get a return on your investment sooner because of the new appeal.
6.   Your probabilities are greater with an address that is available to doing business with suppliers.

Some cons are:
1.   Higher start-up costs.
2.   Higher marketing costs.
3.   Unproven market.
4.   Higher risks.
5.   Added stress in getting utility companies.
6.   Obtaining permits can be time consuming.
7.   Building inspections can be time consuming.

Re-opening an existing location also has its pros and cons as well.
Some pros are:
1.   The area is already recognized.
2.   Established with local agencies
3.   Lower start-up costs.
4.   Inheritance of prior business' successes.

Some cons are:
1.   Inheritance of prior business' problems.
2.   Re-establishing the store is re-opened.
3.   Trying to regain loss market share.

There are many other pros and cons in choosing to do either scenario. Perform an S.W.O.T.T. analysis on that specific market in both cases and determine which route comes out more favorable. If you decide to build-out an existing location, you can use this form. If not, then skip using this form and construct your operational budget.

Build-Out Budget

Use the build-out budget form to bind the contractors' bids to your project and to keep aware of your project's costs. The build-out budget will vary depending on the building, the location and city's requirements. You may incur costs that are not enclosed and you may not have to deal with some of these costs that are listed.

Build-Out Budget
What is needed varies

Items	Vendor/Contractor Name	Initials	Vendor Price Quote
Wall Construction	_____	_____	$_____
Electrical	_____	_____	$_____
Plumbing	_____	_____	$_____
Overhead Signage	_____	_____	$_____
Flooring	_____	_____	$_____
Shelves	_____	_____	$_____
Point of Sale/ Eq	_____	_____	$_____
Fixtures (Mirrors, Store Signs, Office Equipment, Computers, Break Room Supplies, etc)	_____	_____	$_____
Miscellaneous (Price Guns, Safe Stereo, Telephones etc.)	_____	_____	$_____
Grand Opening	_____	_____	$_____

Reason

Items		Initials	Vendor Price Quote
Hidden Costs 1	_____	_____	$_____
Hidden Costs 2	_____	_____	$_____
Hidden Costs 3	_____	_____	$_____
Hidden Costs 4	_____	_____	$_____
Hidden Costs 5	_____	_____	$_____

Total Budget
$_____

Operation Budget

Unlike the Build-Out Budget, the Operation Budget will be a barometer to help determine what your monthly costs will be. Most of these costs are out of your hands and typically unknown until entering into the business. However, this form will help you to get a clearer picture of what costs to expect. Many times we walk into a situation not knowing the total picture and attempting to figure it out once we are in the situation. Some people are able to successfully figure it out once they are in it, while others do not handle those surprises well. This form will make life much easier for you!

Monthly Operation Budget
These steps vary depending on the location and needs

Fixed Costs	Biller's Name	Due Date	Amount
Lease _____	_____	$_____
Telephone_____	_____	$_____
Insurance_____	_____	$_____

Variable Costs	Biller's Name	Due Date	Amount
Electrical_____	_____	$_____
Water_____	_____	$_____
Marketing_____	_____	$_____
Product Ordering_____	_____	$_____
Merchant Fees_____	_____	$_____
Payroll_____	_____	$_____
Taxes_____	_____	$_____
Capital Expenditures/ Business Growth _____	_____	$_____
Office Supplies_____	_____	$_____
Unknowns_____	_____	$_____
Unknowns_____	_____	$_____
Unknowns_____	_____	$_____

Total Budget

$_____

Daily Budget

$_____

**Divide your monthly budget by 30 (30 days) to get your daily sales revenue requirement.

Product Start-Up Budget

You will need to determine how much money will be needed to properly stock your location to avoid the appearance of barely making ends meet or you may not be in business too long. Just to give you an idea of how much funds should be allocated to a specific location use this formula. This is not the standard. It is just a guideline. You will want to budget for roughly $45-$55 per square foot of product in your location. So if your location is 1,400 square feet, then you would want to prepare for $63,000-$77,000 worth of products in your store. There are four departments of products in your store and how you financially divide each department is up to you and your layout and you specialty. You have chemicals, equipment, hair and accessories (hats, fingernail polish, glue, nail clippers, etc.) Use your start-up budget sheet to keep track of how you are disseminating these funds.

Products Start-Up Budget

Products	Distributor	Costs
Chemicals	_____	$_____
Chemicals	_____	$_____
Equipment	_____	$_____
Equipment	_____	$_____
Equipment	_____	$_____
Equipment	_____	$_____
Hair	_____	$_____
Hair	_____	$_____
Hair	_____	$_____
Hair	_____	$_____
Accessories	_____	$_____
Unknowns	_____	$_____
Unknowns	_____	$_____
Unknowns	_____	$_____

Total Budget

$_____

CHAPTER 7
SELECTING A LOCATION

Selecting a Location (Chapter 7)

The first parameter that you must consider when looking for a location is your budget. Since your location will be your most important cost, determining what amount you are comfortable paying is something that should be realistic. Don't make the mistake of picking a location based on your emotions and not its true business potential and your ability to cover the costs. Some locations are overpriced for a particular industry but greatly priced for another. This goes back to your market research and targeted market. Once you are comfortable that the market presence has great revenue potential, then choose a storefront space that will accommodate your budget.

Market Density

As the saying goes, "Location, Location, Location!" As discussed before, you will want to ensure your location is conducive to your market. You want to ensure there is enough market density to support your business. The average person tends to believe that a large number of persons will yield a successful business. Unfortunately, this is not the case. To the naked eye, it may seem that a business may be successful simply because of the market's density. I am sure you have seen businesses that have closed their doors due to a lack of business even though there remains a strong presence of consumers in that market. This is because the market must be studied in order to determine if you would be able to get your piece of the pie. Make certain that your location presents the opportunities for your business to grow. Don't become attached to a certain market because of your emotions. Don't make the mistake of assuming because a particular demographic exists in a market, your business will be lucrative.

The Location

You will want a location that is easily accessible to the main road. The location should also have adequate and visible parking. Since women will be your largest consumer base, you will want to ensure your store's parking lot is free from damage, debris, and loiterers and is well lit. If your store will be anywhere other than an indoor mall, you will want a location that can be seen from the road by drivers. To help this visibility, many strip malls have a large sign marquee with a list of all the strip mall's business occupants. Consider placing your business name or type in this marquee. The business type (beauty supply) will be easier for customers driving by to identify what your store carries, rather than them trying to interpret this by your store's name. Ensure the location you select is proportioned to carry a large variety of products. Most locations will be boxes. The location should be wide enough and deep enough to accommodate customers and products. The ceilings should also be at lease 8 feet. This will allow enough room for you to display posters and other paraphernalia.

Market Saturation

Market Saturation is depicted as how many businesses are operating in the immediate area. To put it in simple terms, how stiff is the competition. Well, even this statement is not that simple. The competition may be stiff because the market density is low or the store may be monopolizing the particular market for a lengthy period of time. You will want to survey the area to ensure your entrance into the market will not be too difficult.

Next, determine whether the Market Life Cycle is at its Introduction, Growth or at its stable Maturity phase. When you can determine at what stage this market is in, then you can determine if it is a risky market. Some areas are undergoing gentrification and this usually changes the dynamics of an area. Be careful to determine if there is any rezoning due to occur in the local market. This typically happens when the market is at its Decline phase in the Life Cycle. A good barometer that a market has been determined to be a good location for business is when large franchises begin developing in that area. Franchises perform due diligence in market research and only develop based off of empirical data rather than emotional decisions or a hunch.

A saturated market can make entering the market very difficult. In some areas of Atlanta, there are stores on every corner. Then in other areas of Atlanta, there are none for miles. You will want to seek out a location that is growing, with a dense population of your target and cost favorable to you as a first time beauty supply owner. If you are a seasoned business owner, then the risks may be a little lower. But for someone who has not experienced the ups and downs that a business may produce coupled with a strong presence of competition or a declining market, seeking a saturated location may not be the best choice. Nonetheless, once you've established that a particular location works for you, then move forward with it.

Sending the Proposal

In many cases, the procedure for creating dialogue between yourself and the property managers is to initiate a telephone call. Be prepared to send a "letter of intent" (LOI) also referred to as a proposal. When you make the phone call, ensure you tell them your name and the company you are calling from. The company, of course, is the one you just created and registered with your local Secretary of State. They will be able to now find your company in the search with the Secretary of State. Good feeling huh? Don't start feeling too warm and fuzzy yet. There's still more work that needs to take place.

While speaking with the property manager, they will be determining from your answers to their questions whether or not they are willing to take the chance and lease you their location. If they do not seem to be attempting to validate your stature, I would be skeptical about doing business with them. Property managers usually seek a five-year commitment (lease) from businesses and they would not want to have a vacant location within a year or two after your business opening. So do not take their screening of you personally. I would actually take it favorable knowing that they plan to do their part to keep you as a tenant in their building. If you pass the telephone checkpoint, it will be time to send your LOI.

Your LOI will need to be brief and to the point. Once it has a clear overview, the property manager will construct a lease agreement to begin negotiations. Here's a sample LOI:

ABC Beauty Supply, LLC
1234 Williams St
Anywhere, US 12345

January 1, 20xx

To: XYZ Enterprises, LLC
c/o Property Manager
5678 Mitchell Road
Anywhere, US 67890

From: ABC Beauty Supply, LLC
1234 Williams St
Anywhere, US 12345

Re: Letter of Intent

(Location Name) Occupancy

This letter serves as intent and notification to your establishment
that ABC Beauty Supply, LLC is interested in occupying suite xxx
in (Location Name) for the purpose of opening a beauty supply store
that will retail cosmetics, hair and nail supplies. We look forward to
working with you. Please forward all correspondence to my
attention at:

ABC Beauty Supply, LLC
1234 Williams St
Anywhere, US 12345
Ph:000-000-0000
Fax: 000-000-0000

Thanks in advance for your cooperation!

Lisa Black
President
ABC Beauty Supply, LLC

Reviewing the Lease

This is a step that you will want to consult with an attorney. There are many legal jargons that are written into leases that can confuse the average person. There are some things in the lease that you will need to pay particular attention to such as understanding your responsibilities as a tenant. Leases are contracts that are written to favor the party who constructs the lease. Know that the terms in the lease will be to protect the developer of the lease but are conditions that you will be able to operate your business under.

Keep in mind that leases are not etched in stone. They are negotiable. If the lease as presented to you has unsatisfactory conditions, do not panic. Simply consult your attorney because leases can be altered to suit your needs. Your attorney will be looking for the lease to contain legal guidelines not specific location guidelines. For example, unless the attorney visits the location to see what hazards are present or other negotiations need to be made, you will need to present your findings to the attorney to have him/her negotiate with the landlord. You will want to inspect the suite for damages that should be repaired by the landlord and have them pay for the repairs or offset the cost to move-in. Ensure the suite has current and operable fixtures as they will help to reduce your insurance costs.

Another clause you will want written in your lease is to have the exclusive rights to sell cosmetic supplies. This will restrict the landlord from leasing to any competitors and forbid another business in that building from selling what you sell. Sometimes other business will want to get a piece of your action by selling items that you carry. Salons, barbershops, spas and nail shops would be typical businesses that would make this attempt.

Don't be surprised if the property manager asks for a guarantor. A guarantor is someone who is responsible for the lease payments in the event the business terminates the lease. New businesses are usually required to produce a guarantor. Study your Common Area Maintenance (CAM) costs, if there are any, to affirm that you are comfortable with any increases. Once you and your attorney have agreed that the lease is suitable for you to sign, get your business license from your local government agency and begin the build-out procedures.

Build-Out Steps
These steps vary depending on the location and needs

While managing these steps, to maximize your costs, make purchases when that step is ready to commence. For example, do not order your products before the floor is installed. This will have your product sitting on the sideline with your funds tied up waiting to make the return on your investment (ROI). This process is called "Just-In Time" (JIT). We will discuss this further, later in the book.

1.   Establish Budget – Determine the amount of cost you can comfortably spend on building out, excluding products

2.   Solicit contractor bids – You want to do this early enough to check references, research work history and make changes in your contractor selection.

3.   Get layout design plans – You can do the draft yourself and have a contractor draw it to code.

4.   Submit plans to appropriate agency in order to obtain permits – This is a process out of your control and cannot be expedited by you. Therefore you need to submit your plans as early as possible.

5.   Order overhead sign – This is a process that can also utilize a lot of time. Speak to your landlord about signage requirements.

6.   Submit plans (design and overhead signage) to landlord – Some landlords require this step and some do not.

7.   Order utilities (including telephone) – You will need your business legal documents in order to get the utilities in the business' name.

8.   Begin the flooring – In most areas, flooring is not a permit requirement. If it is not, get this work done.

Once you receive the permits, execute steps 9 & 10

9.   Build store layout, start plumbing, start electrical – Do the work simultaneously, this will help to expedite the process. (Be careful not to begin a project that has a prerequisite of another project.)

10. Get inspections – There are draft inspections and final inspections needed to complete the entire project. Get inspections as project permits.

Manage all work (electrical, plumbing, mechanical, environmental, if applicable)

11. Setup VISA, MasterCard, AMEX, Discover, processing accounts

12. Purchase credit card terminal and Pin-pad

13. Order you point of sale equipment – There are different types of point of sales. You can go fully automated for a few thousand dollars or you can purchase a basic cash register for $100. Bare in mind, you get what you pay for.

14. Get final inspections

- If all inspections pass, apply for "certificate of occupancy"

15. Move on to implementing operations budget plan.

CHAPTER 8
SETTING UP
YOUR STORE

Setting Up Your Store (Chapter 8)

The Store Layout

Congratulations! It's now time to set-up your store. Before doing the design, establish where your exits are. In order to pass a fire inspection, your exits must be clearly marked and free from obstruction. Next, determine the location of your main exit. You will want your point of sale located on the way toward the exit. This will allow you the ability to ensure no additional items were picked up after the customer completes their sale transaction. It will all also allow you to query the customer to find out if their needs were met if they are approaching the exit without making a purchase and this placement will also allow you to properly acknowledge the customer as they leave even if they have not made a purchase. Once these exits and locations are determined, you can begin the store design.

Remember in your design you are attempting to accomplish multiple things:

1.   You want to display and store the products.

2.   You want your store's layout able to help market and sell products. In this case, the shelves and displays will be positioned where the customer can properly browse the store without confusion or tediousness.

3.   You want the store to not present any blind spots. This will help to deter the possibility of theft.

4.   You want your displays to be arranged safely and securely. There are individuals who shop stores to find hazards in order to cash in on your negligence.

5.   You want to maximize on your space. Just like the world we live in, there is no more real estate available.

This reason causes for an appreciation in property value. View your store as the same concept. Whatever space you have is all that will be given (even if there are expansion opportunities). You will not want to purchase shelves that extend too much into the aisle because this will minimize the number of total aisles you will be able to have in your store. Most provinces have a width minimum restriction so don't assume that if you can comfortably walk the aisles mean it is enough space. Check with your local authorities.

You will want your store to be uniformed. You don't want to have mismatched displays and shelving. This will present an unprofessional look and may reduce your probability of gaining a repeat customer. Customers like to feel comfortable where they spend their monies. Don't you? When you design your store layout and begin to purchase display items, be critical of your decisions. Do not think with your emotional checkbook. The customer could care less if your finances were tight. If they are, you may be embarking on opening a store too soon or you may want to consider downgrading your store size or location.

You will need to have reserve funds on-hand for several months in order to ensure all costs are covered. Keep in mind that your displays should allow for modifications as your inventory grows. I know storeowners that have minced costs severely on the construction of their stores and their customer retention became extremely low. Not saying this is the sole cause of the store's inability to retain customers, but while I view these stores from a customer' point of view, I believe it contributed. Customers often feel like owners are not investing into their community long-term if they do not witness signs of reinvestment into their businesses. Plus, it can be perceived as a struggling business, which customers tend to shy away from. Be careful. Being too cautious can cause a catastrophe.

You will want to be able to view your aisles from the point of sale area. This will not only help you to maintain store security, it can also allow you to help customers by being able to direct them to the products from where you are working. It gives you multi-tasking abilities and the capability to assist multiple customers at one time.

Your security cameras should be placed to clearly view the point of sale, and the products. Placing cameras in the corners of the store is always a good idea. This gives the camera a nice panoramic view of the store. This is especially essential when you only have a few cameras to begin with.

You will want to decorate the store. Give it a ladies' touch. If you are a male opening a store like myself, find yourself a female quickly. Men tend to get to the point and forget about the bells and whistles. However, as you decorate keep in mind that it is a commercial location and not a residence. The décor must be able to withstand high traffic volume without disrupting the appearance of the store. For example, you will not want to carpet your floor with Persian Carpeting. There will be rainy days that will attract mud. The carpet will not last. Think about this. Your store will see thousands of customers per year and even more that will not make a purchase. Therefore, you will have to keep a clean store for those window shoppers that add to the wear and tear of your store but not to your profit margin. Unfortunately, this is one of those bitter costs of doing business. There will be more.

Hanging posters is always great advertisement. The manufacturers and distributors will be happy to assist you with obtaining some. Tastefully hang them throughout the store and in your windows. (There are also signage restrictions for window displays. Check with your local government.) If you have store policies such as, not accepting checks or no cash refunds display those signs as well.

Placing the Products

"There was once a small thing that turned into a huge thing because of advertising." (Mark Twain) Never pass the opportunity to market your products. This is the concept that you will want to implement when you are placing your products on the shelves and in the displays. Placing the products in the stores is not as simple as just placing them in alphabetical order or numerical order. Your products should be placed where it makes sense. When a customer is in the store, your store should be able to sell itself. Selling itself is by allowing the shelves to cross, sub and/or up-sell. We will discuss these functions in subsequent chapters. The store should be laid out with shopping ease. You will want to place items that have the same use in the same area. For example, you will not want to place hair relaxers with nail polishes. You will want to place the shampoos with the conditioners. You will want to place the relaxers with the bases. You will want to place bump fighting products with the shaving products. You get my drift. By doing this, you spark interest for the customer to get the additional item that goes with the one they may have visited your store to solely purchase.

There are also some customers that will enter your store who are not in a conversational mood or who are shy. Even though you would want to brighten their day or get them to open up, some shoppers would prefer to find items on their own. Simply help them out with placing the items uncomplicatedly. You want the products to silently speak to the customer. You want to have the items **"fronted and faced"**. This means you want the products sitting to the closest front edge of the shelf and the labels facing to the front. This small theory dispels the employees are taking pride in their store. Or you can invest in "automatic fronting shelves". These shelves have a retractable arm behind the products that will push the line of items forward as one item is picked up off of the shelf.

Have you ever visited someone's home and it smells and it is a pigpen? When you enter, you may not tend to show much respect for the home. I remember growing up where one of my friend's homes was deemed the neighborhood hangout. The sitting area had little furnishings and the house was rugged looking on the inside. You were able to traffic in and out of the home and you had no inclining to perhaps wipe your feet at the door. We played video games all day, ate and drank as we pleased and even invited persons to the home that the residents didn't know. This was also okay. Though there was adult supervision there, there was an absence of rules. Then we would go next door to the house sitting right beside it and the atmosphere alone influenced us to wipe our feet, sit correctly in the furniture, which by the way was clean and the floors were free from debris. Entering a facility can set the tone for the behavior of an individual. This is not a fail-safe remedy but it helps and expresses showmanship.

Some stores simply place the entire product lines together. This is also a good idea. If the customer is loyal to a particular product, placing the entire line together can introduce the customer to more of the manufacturers' products. This is a great concept. There are other concepts such as category placement. You can arrange our store by categories, meaning you can put all gels, greases and/or hair oils together no matter the manufacturer. When you setup the store, you should have a balanced thought about doing so.

What should be placed high on shelves? What should be placed low on shelves? Remember you want to run a safe operation. Remember OSHA (Occupational Safety and Health Administration)? You will want to have a safe environment, not only for your customers but for your employees as well. So you will want to place your larger items low and the less hazardous items at eye level or above reach minimizing the danger of a large item falling from the shelf. You still want to determine which item goes at eye level and what items go just below or above eye level. Attractive items or items that you want to have high volume sales should be right at eye level, between 5'5" and 5'8". You want these items to jump off the shelf at the shopper.

If you will be selling a variety of wigs, you will want to place the display wigs up high on glass shelving. You will want your shopper to be able to have a clear view of your display wigs. You can be creative with the displaying of the wigs. You can place them in categories by the type or by the color. There are full wigs and half wigs (express weaves). You can place these wigs in one section then go a step further and place them by color and styles. There are a large variety of colors. There are a large variety of styles. You have short cuts, curls (tight, loose), flips and more. Placing them in categories will help you or your employees be able to direct a customer to the particular wig that they are seeking or to better identify what wig the customer is looking for without having to reach for the wig.

You will want to place the expensive and fragile items out of the customers' reach. Once your store opens, you will have a good idea of the behavioral habits of your customers. We've had stores in different markets. As different as the markets, so are the differences in the customers. In one market, the customers are more outlandish than the other. Though the customers are not bad acting, they are a little more aggressive and less careful when they are browsing the store. Because of this, we are not able to place easily breakable items within reach of the customers. Your popular items that are easy to be concealed should also be placed where the customer must ask for your assistance.

You will also want your checkout area to be a "check me out" area. You will want your customers to "check-out" grab items and samples. This is where you want to place the low-cost items that are attractive to the customers. A customer would add a $1.00 item to their ticket without many complaints. This is called impulse spending. You want your customers to purchase these *convenient* items. Some of these items are purse sized lip-glosses, vehicle air fresheners, etc. Often times, the customers' eyes are roaming while they are checking out at the point of sale to determine whether or not they forgot something or to see if there is anything else they can use. Maximize on the product placement for a better shopping experience for the customer.

CHAPTER 9
LAYING THE
FOUNDATION FOR
OPERATIONS

Laying the Foundation for Operations (Chapter 9)

Company Policies

✶ You can construct your own company/store policies as long as they are within reason and legal. Some business owners would commission an outside agency to handle this task. It is truly up to your preference. If you are a totally new business owner you may want to seek the assistance of a business consultant or business development manager. However, the consultant will not be the one running your business on a day-to-day basis so I would recommend you not totally withdraw yourself from this task.

Policies are in place for a reason. Sometimes they are in place for safety reasons, security reasons or loss prevention reasons. You will need to have a clear vision of what level and intensity you expect your business operations to run and construct your policies according to this vision. The reason for this is you want to revisit your company policies as little as possible. If you develop your company policies and never have to make modifications to it, this means the policies was clear and well thought out to meet your overall vision and objectives. To the contrary, revisiting your company policies does not necessarily mean you did not do a good job constructing it, sometimes unforeseen circumstances may arise that were not thought about originally.

Depending on your location and type of clientele, your company policies may vary. If you are doing a lot of business around companies that are also doing business with you, there may be a high level of checks wanting to be written. If your store has a no-check policy, this may inconvenience some of the owners of your local businesses such as salons and barbershops. Checks were developed to minimize individuals carrying a large sum of cash and other reasons, but unfortunately those persons who truly had no monies in their account, prompted many business owners to refuse taking checks because some have abused check writing. Fortunately, there are solutions to this problem. There are companies that handle any delinquent checks for your business for a monthly fee. These companies guarantee your funds and refund the money to you and they take on the tedious task of pursuing the bad check writers.

There is also the issue of refunds. Since the floodgates for giving refunds with no questions asked have been offered to the public by large retail chains, shoppers of smaller retail stores also expect you to do the same. The difference between the smaller stores and the large chains is the volume disparity. Larger retail stores are often more liquid than a smaller store. They can also withstand taking a much larger amount of losses. Most of these stores are also publicly traded, giving them a greater advantage with their cash flow.

What it boils down to is this... the customer could care less about this disparity and are usually only concerned with the end result, getting their refund. You will have to question yourself as to whether you can provide refunds, offer store credits or implement "all sales are final." The latter option can work for you or against you. The pro is you will know that whatever is sold is truly sold. The con is you can lose customers as the customers see your location as an inconsiderate way of doing business. Like I said, depending on your market, you will have to determine how strict your policies can be. Your store policy can simply be only you the owner or a manager can process returns. Some stores go as far as only allowing a certain number of youngsters in the store at one time and even making each customer place all bags at the counter before entering the aisles. In my opinion, typically, if you treat people like criminals, animals or second-class, that's how they tend to act. You may have one or two that even being treated with respect acts disrespectfully but that is not the norm. Think about it and make the necessary implementations.

There are many other rules to consider in your policy book especially if you will have employees. Here are a few to consider:

- ◆ Opening and Closing Procedures
- ◆ Return Policy
- ◆ Exchange Policy
- ◆ Retail Operations Policy
- ◆ Employee Conduct
  - ○ (Insubordination, Sexual Harassment, Right to Work, Intoxication, Stealing, Personal Visits)
- ◆ Vacation Policy
- ◆ Bereavement Policy

- ◆ Time-Off (Unexcused Absences)
- ◆ Sick Time
- ◆ Dereliction of Duty
- ◆ Equipment Usage
- ◆ Discounts
- ◆ Violence
- ◆ Emergency Procedures
- ◆ Solicitation
- ◆ 3rd Party Information
- ◆ Company Information Disclosure

These are just some rules to get your brain working. Think on all of the situations that you believe may have a possibility of happening. See the good and perhaps the bad occurring.

Marketing

You will also want to lie out policies for how you handle your marketing. You will want to offer discounts, specials, coupons, samples, grand opening (one-time event) and customer appreciation day, week or month. With marketing, you want to have a marketing plan. This plan must be budgeted and coordinated. There are times of the year when individuals want to purchase certain items. For example, wintertime is a higher wig purchase season while the summer time customers flock towards the braided hair. This concept is similar to customers purchasing shorts for the summer and jackets for the winter. You will want to have a forecasted plan in place for marketing particular items to the market.

Discounts
You want to offer discounts to people in the industry. Why? They have the power to offer credibility on your business to their clientele as well. Give them the incentive to do so.

Specials
Have specials being offered to the general public during your predetermined time(s). This will give them an incentive to visit your location for the first time and maybe become a regular patron to your business.

✱ Coupons

Build a customer database. Know your customers and offer them coupons. Let them know their bucks are being reinvested in their pockets as kickbacks. Coupons are a very useful way of sustaining and even increasing your sales volume.

✱ Samples

Samples are given to you for free so pass on the savings! Some stores I've visited attempted to charge me for samples that I KNOW they received for free. Never stereotype a customer. Never judge who you may think they are. They may seem like an "Average Joe Blow" but in fact could be a Chamber of Commerce board member heading home from the gym. Pass your savings on to your customers and do not try to undermine them.

Grand Opening (Customer Appreciation)

As you saw in your start-up budget sheet, this should be incorporated in your expenses. This should be a part of your costs and a part of your policy. Have regular customer appreciation times, whether they are days, weeks or months throughout the year. Make this a part of your marketing costs.

CHAPTER 10
PRICING TO SELL, SELLING TO PRICE

Pricing to Sell, Selling to Price (Chapter 10)

Before discussing "pricing", let's first understand making a profit. Even though making a profit is a popular topic and the number one priority of business, many new (and sometimes seasoned) entrepreneurs do not fully understand what constitutes a profit and what all to consider in the costs in order to properly price their products.

Who absorbs profit? Who pays for profit? "Profit" in our society has become something that many organizations desire. Even in Government. The Government refers to profit as "surplus". As this profit is sought and handed to each entity, (customer distributor, wholesaler, retailer, consumer), what happens next? Well, it is added on top of the cost then handed to the buyer of the product as *their* cost. The buyer then prices their goods or services (with this purchasing cost included) and seeks to earn their "profit". This entity then does the same. At some point it stops and it is always with the consumer; this is the person who actually uses the product without using it to deliver another product. A cost is what a buyer purchases and a price is what a seller sells. In other words, a cost is liability and a price is an asset. If it is your price, it means you are selling it. If it is a cost, it means you are buying it. If it remains a product, it remains a cost therefore you never price it. This means that you are perhaps the consumer, the end user of the product.

As the American System evolves, more and more entities enter the market (and distribution channel) to deliver a product associated with an original product. For example, "OnStar" has now entered the automobile industry and has become a "cost" for GM (General Motors). GM then calls it a feature, increases the price of their product (the automobile), and pass it to the consumer as a new price in order to maintain their profit margin they had before the OnStar feature; not overall profit in the dollar amount but rather in the percentage amount. This can be deadly to the American Economy as the prices of goods and services are rapidly increasing faster than the salary of workers and faster than entirely new industries can be sustainably created; though they bring many conveniences. Trucking Companies get involved with bringing the product to the market and now "*Transportation*" has become a cost in delivering goods across the world when previously, business was typically done locally because transportation was a very expensive cost during industrialization. With these minimal shipping costs to the distributor, retailer or consumer, they sustained profits. Within *Transportation*, liability insurance, tolls, taxes, fuel, vehicle maintenance and other costs have become affiliated with delivering the products. Duplicate this scenario with many other industries that enter into an existing one and you will see how burdensome the "profit" can be to the consumer or taxpayer but very beneficial to business owners who run efficient operations. The creation of jobs can be deadly to an economy if those created jobs are entering to now *share* the already existing profit if there is not a strong scalable demand for that industry. You can expect higher costs of goods and services and other side effects but this is part of Capitalism; free open enterprising, risks and rewards.

If everyone continues to become a beneficiary of the profits in a handful of market industries where demand is soft, industrialization can crumble. The debt of the American person will continue to rise and so will the debt of the Government. Entities borrow money in order to be able to acquire the cost of their seller, if they are unable to move their product or service in huge volume in short spans of time, their profit will not be "true profit". You will simply see a deferred "costs" called a loan on their balance sheet. Let's not add the sunken or hidden costs a company is desperate to recoup, whether from failed marketing campaigns or failed products. It doesn't just disappear. Someone pays the cost for it. You may find it to be the consumer. Don't let me discourage your aspirations. I am an entrepreneur to heart. This illustration is to get your mind wrapped around the concept that running effective and efficient businesses is what leads to wealthy retirement. Not implementing a robust plan that is properly researched is often any new entrepreneur's downfall.

Many jobs are created and many payrolls are met using loans in hopes that a "*true profit*" can be realized. Our economy has revealed the truth about many businesses' financial position in the market and what really happens to a profit. Cost is like a burden you don't want to carry. The person who is left with it last is the person that relieves the pressure from everyone else.

So as you price your products understand... **What's in a profit? Who absorbs it? What are the side effects of it?**

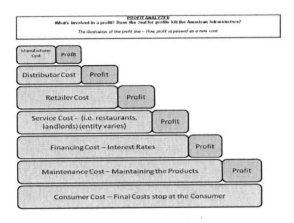

Pricing

Price your products in order to make sales. Make sales so you can set your true price! Sometimes we are forced to start our stores at different prices. Sometimes it is due to competition in the area and sometimes it is due to non-familiarity with a good product. I briefly touched on pricing strategies earlier but let's go in-depth this time around.

Pricing to make sales would be attached to the "Sales" pricing strategy. This means, you want to set your product at a low price to make a high number of sales. Not profit, just sales. This strategy is to get a high number of persons through the door and purchase items. This strategy is usually when a business would like a high number of visitors. Sometimes this is the only motive, to simply generate traffic volume, which would lead to profits but not a large profit margin.

There are other motives as well. Selling to price! Selling to price is the second motive behind pricing to make a high number of sales. There are businesses that sell at a low price to gain the demand of the market and then as the demand increases so does the price. You will want to be able to capitalize on the best profit margin possible but sometimes this short-term strategy is the way to gain the long-term profits.

There are other reasons as well. It is called the leading loss. Let's recapture the objectives of the different strategies.

Pricing Objectives

- Sales - to increase the number of purchases. This strategy is when the items are priced low to appeal to the interest and sale to the customers. This strategy often yields the lowest profit margin but also often yields the highest market share through a high traffic count.

- Profit – this strategy is in place to maximize the amount of profit that each sale obtains. This is often the case with trendy products. Take the DVD player for example. When this device was first introduced to the market it cost hundreds of dollars. Now after several years, you can get a DVD player for as little as $69. It's still the same device, however the manufacturers of DVD players were able to maximize on the early sales gaining higher profits with each sale. Since offering new products to the market is risky, the sale is usually profit-based in case the product is not widely accepted. Once it is accepted and technology continues to revolutionize, the prices tend to drop.

- Status Quo – Status Quo is following the norm. It's often a big risk going against the norm of anything. But with big risks, come big rewards. Pricing for the status quo is the safest route in opening a new business. It would cut down on any potential customer complaints especially in a high competitive market. If you want to quietly gain the trust and appeal to the customer, study your market and price accordingly. This is Status Quo.

Knowing these different strategies is very important to the success of your business. Since first impressions are lasting impressions, you will not want to give off a bad first impression that may spread throughout the social circle of the shoppers that visited your store. Only you as the proprietor have the full spectrum view of what your business can sustain. Where did your funds come from to start the business? How strong is the competition in your market? What is your patience level? How long can you wait to see profits or to break-even? The answers to these questions are indicators of where your pricing should lie.

There is one thing to bear in mind. You will carry thousands of products. Your pricing strategy will not be a blanket of the entire store. Although you may have competition in your market, they may not carry a particular product that you carry allowing your pricing strategy to be different on that product. For that product you may be able to use the Profit Pricing strategy and for other items in your store you may only be able to stick within the Status Quo Pricing strategy. You may be able to implement different strategies simply on the category of the item you are selling, chemicals, accessories, hair and wigs or you will have to narrow it down further to determine if different strategies are necessary between the varied chemical manufacturers and so on. Don't look for an easy formula to price your entire store. Go a step beyond that and learn what the market can withstand and what your store can offer.

There is such a thing called the "leading loss". The leading loss is a concept that business owners typically do not relish. The leading loss happens when a business sells a product for a loss simply because the market cannot withstand its true retail price with the hopes of cross-selling an item with the loss leader and make the profit on that cross-sold item. For example, Best Buy may sell a plasma television at a loss but sells the customer a warranty that will be the counteraction of the loss. Sometimes this formula is necessary depending on the location of the store and the product being offered. At times you may need to implement this strategy in hopes of moving a product.

Selling

Do you recall episodes on television where one couple goes to another couples home for dinner and the visiting husband or wife gets offended and before storming out of the house they yell to their spouse, "C'mon dear, we're leaving!" Once the spouse decides to leave with the other one, this is a way to view the cross-selling technique. Before the customer leaves the store, they should be taking an item with them that goes with what they purchased.

Although your store's inventory may contain thousands of items and its value will be worth tens of thousands, the list of types of items in your store will be a short one. You should have shampoos, texturizers, body lotion, greases, and so on. You should get my drift. Now, among those items, you have categories of what that item does and its value. Some items costs more and some items may say it does more or does a specific thing. One shampoo may be a neutralizing shampoo and another shampoo may be a moisturizing shampoo. Then there are brands that go with these specific shampoos. There are shampoos that costs as little as $.99 then you have others as high as $20, depending on the brand, of course. Comprehending this makes implementing the two of the three sales strategies easier for you.

Cross selling is a technique where the salesperson suggests the customer purchases an item that goes with their original purchase. Bankers use this technique quite often. When a customer opens, let's say a checking account, the banker offers the customer a savings account, checks and sometimes depending on how receptive the customer is, they offer them life insurance policies, mutual funds and other bank offerings. If we revert back to the leading loss example, cross selling is the only technique that makes selling the item for a loss worthwhile. This is something that should be a basic principle in the sales of your products.

The other strategy is called the up selling technique. This technique is offering a product of better quality and higher value to the customer. Some customers would visit a beauty supply store every week to purchase weaving hair. Offering them a higher quality type of hair could allow the customer a longer grace period between hair purchases. The same goes for bump fighting products. There are products that cost much more than others but the benefit of its long lasting action make the product a better choice. This strategy can increase the store's profit margin and improve the cash flow of the store. Up selling can also increase customer satisfaction. Many of us use the price as a barometer when we are shopping and often disregard quality and long lasting effects of the product.

The final strategy is sub-selling. Sub-selling is a technique that should rarely be used. Why? Because one important factor in customer satisfaction is always having the product on hand. Nevertheless, it's a technique that must be understood. Sub-selling is selling a different product in the place of another. This should only happen when the store is out of stock on the item the customer is attempting to purchase or if you are recommending a product that may produce better results than that of the one the customer originally came to purchase. I would not recommend another product in the place of another if it were in stock unless you are totally confident and sure that you are making a well-informed decision. Knowing this gives you the advantage in being able to offer a similar item in its place knowing that the customer will get "like" results as if they purchased the product that you are out of.

All of these strategies are only effective when the employee is fully aware of the products and how they work. If the employees do not know the products well, the sales revenue will reflect it. Customers will not continue to visit your location if they feel that informed employees are not serving them. You will want to train yourself and your employees on the total operations of your store especially the products and sales strategies. When serving a customer, you will want to employ at the minimum one of these three techniques, if not two at a time, the cross selling and up selling. If you are not totally apt on sales functions I would suggest you get with a sales consultant or purchase a reputable sales book.

CHAPTER 11
GETTING YOUR
STAFF

Getting Your Staff (Chapter 11)

Selecting Your Employees

Some owners are not able to initially hire employees upon opening. If you are in the position to do so, wonderful! If you are capable of doing so but not able to pay the big bucks join the many business owners in the territory; caught between a rock and a hard place. Many employers need the assistance of employees to build a strong and smooth operation but they seldom possess the capital in order to hire the best of the best. This causes a higher turnover rate of employees.

This chapter will outline some helpful tips. If you are or have been in a hiring capacity for retail operations, then you should be well on your way to hiring bright employees.

The selection process can be tedious. One thing you will want to keep in mind with employees is their motives are totally different from yours. When an employer hires an employee, they expect to make money from the employees' skills. Meanwhile, the employee is thinking about making money from the employer. With these two different perspectives, there are often growing pains in the relationship. These growing pains can be minimized if the employer is very careful in their selection.

If your career track has been being an employee, this is when your ideology of the workplace will have to change. Even managers in corporations are not in the same capacity of an entrepreneur. Imagine going to your job as a marketing director one day and your boss pulls you into his office and states that the business is reorganizing and you will not have to actively manage human resources, accounts payables and receivables, operations, shipping and receiving, inventory management, payroll, customer service and quality control departments. How would you feel? Would you embrace her proposition?

This is what an entrepreneur is faced with daily. When going into business for yourself, never assume the hard work is over! This is when the work *actually* begins. You will have to possess what I refer to as the 3 sights... foresight, insight and hindsight. You will want to have a panoramic view of your business being able to identify changes that need to be made and the ability to zone in on the small infractions that require adjustments. Hiring employees definitely requires a sharpened view!

I would urge you to keep one thing in mind. If you have a relative that is a poor performer at their job, be leery of bringing them to work for your business. Many times, your relative(s) can be a poor performer and just because they are related to you don't expect that you will definitely make their performance change once they are employed by you. Mixing family with business can be a very risky thing. Your relatives often simply see you as their relative regardless whether or not you are now their employer and their boss. Do not select with your emotions. Select with evidence. Ensure the person you decide to entrust with your money and investment has a proven track record of a good work ethic, dependability and integrity.

Once a new business is finally open, the floodgates open for applicants. Don't be too quick to hire to fill a simple need. (In many states, it is much easier to hire than to fire. Know your state's labor laws.) You can get a good idea of who you would like to hire based on their initial contact that they make with you. If your operation seems small or obscure to the applicant their level of respect will reflect in how they address you. Evidence will be in their attitude and appearance. You will have a lot more kinks to work out when your business opens and adding an employee with low potential is not a good idea.

The Interview

The interview is the opportune time to determine if an employee cuts the mustard. However it is not 100% guaranteed. Some individuals give great first impressions and good con men/women typically know how to con the smartest individuals. However, there are small telltale signs that you can pick up on.

- Appearance
- Attention Span
- Mannerism
- Punctuality
- Track Record
- References

These are a few interview questions you may want to ask.

1. What is your reason for leaving your previous job?
2. Tell me one of your weaknesses.
3. What type of experience do you have?
4. Why should I hire you?
5. What skills will you bring to the business to make it run better?

While asking these questions, you will want to observe the applicant's demeanor. Often times, they are not expecting the interviewer to be so direct in their questioning. When direct questions are asked and the applicant does not have a favorable answer, they will fiddle or stall before giving their response. Do not just interview the applicant seeking verbal responses. You will also want to seek non-verbal (body language) responses as well. A person's demeanor can sometimes speak much louder and more honest than the verbal responses we may seek.

The applicant's personality should also be conducive to your vision. Since ordinary business owners all share the same vision, you should already know what type of personality you would be looking for in your applicant. Your employees will need to be personable and able to interact with a wide range of consumers. You will not want an employee who can only relate with individuals of their age, race, sex, etc. Your establishment should be inviting to a varied type of persons. Since your inventory will have thousands of different products, you can expect to have thousands of different customers too. The personality should be professional, courteous, understanding and pleasant. Whatever you ask of your employees, you need to set the example. Be professional, courteous, understanding and pleasant.

Your applicant must also be trainable. Analyzing their previous work history should give you a good idea of whether or not they are able to adjust and fit in well in your operations. If you decide to hire them, ensure you give them sufficient training for their position. Never take for granted that an employee knows their job. Always ensure you train them to be effective and efficient. Multi-tasking is required in this business and they should be able to handle multiple tasks and even multiple customers. Seek employees that possess this innate capability.

Know your employment laws of your state. Hire according to laws of your state. Ensure your employees are legal to work in your establishment. You can verify a person's social security number by calling (800) 772-6270. Be familiar with EEOC, OSHA, Fair Labor Standards Act, FMLA Act, USERRA, EEO, Unemployment Insurance, Child Labor Laws – (in case you hire any part-time high school students) and other agencies' requirements of your state. Know your market and compensate accordingly. You will want to log onto www.salary.com in order to get a comparison of the market's salaries in your industry. This will give you a good barometer to start from with a compensation package. If you want to offer health benefits you can inquire with your retail insurance company. They will sometimes offer health benefits.

You can select your pay period and paydays. Determine a payday that would work in your favor. There are affordable payroll processing companies that can handle the paying of your employees. This may be a good idea if you are not well versed in payroll taxes and deductions. You will still have control of the wages and schedule of pay for the employee. You will submit the information to the processing company and they will handle the rest. However, hiring a payroll processing company is not imperative. Not doing so will not make or break your business. It all depends on how well you are running your operation.

CHAPTER 12
WE ARE HERE TO
SERVE YOU

We Are Here to Serve You (Chapter 12)

Customer Service

Customer Service has recently become a major force in the success of a business. This has become the cornerstone of a business simply because of increased competition giving customers increased options. The tables have turned in business whereas customers are now empowered.

Keep in mind, you want to employ customer service and customer focused employees. We often carry our emotions into business situations and act according to the way we personally feel rather than act according to what benefits the establishment. Yes. We are servants and should carry ourselves as such. Now, millions of you reading this book may disagree with being a servant or put up a resistance at being a servant but this is what drives customer service ...being a customer servant. Being a servant does not necessarily mean being a slave. It means serving your customer's needs and doing so with joy and a sense of urgency.

When your customer is unable to find a product in your store, don't just point and send the customer to the product unless you are in the middle of multi-tasking. If a task or helping another customer is preventing you from personally escorting the customer to the product, point out the location with politeness and joy. Your first instinct should be to always escort the customer to the item. Your second instinct should be to reach items for the customer that they cannot reach with joy and urgency.

You do not want to bring your personal issues into the store, check them at the door. Many businesses suffer because of personal attitudes residing in the business and these attitudes shape the culture of the business. Avoid giving a customer unsolicited advice! Leave it up to them to ask for your opinion. You do not want your business to be seen as having a poor or negative organizational culture. You and your employees should be asking, "How may I serve you today?" You want to be able to predict and fulfill the customer's needs. You don't want to just be a person who resells products. You want the ambience of your establishment calming and comfortable for the customer.

Ambience

Five Senses
Ambience is created through the five senses: hearing, seeing smelling touching, and tasting (figuratively):

Hearing
Your customer should be able to withstand what they are hearing in your business. This means your speech should be profanity-free, your tone should be relative and not condescending and your music should be soothing. True, you may have customers that are overbearing, filled with profanity and obnoxious, however even they would welcome a good atmosphere if you present it. The name of the game is to appeal to a wide range of individuals. So remember, you want to have music that anyone can listen to and conversation that will not run-off or offend anyone.

(*Caution* – *Don't attempt to be double-minded trying to appeal to different customers by switching your behavior based on who is in your store. Imagine if two of your regular but different customers are in the store at the same time? One will be turned off by your difference in behavior*).

Seeing
Let's talk about seeing. Customers want to see a clean store and clean employees. If you present a messy and junky look you give the impression that you are not taking much pride in your business and if you are not taking pride in your business, then why should the customer? You will want to provide a dress code for yourself and your employees. You will want to keep your store clean. You want to keep your items clean. You will want to keep your items fronted and faced. It is not a tough job to do.

Smelling
Have you ever entered an establishment and smelled a foul odor? Did that odor linger with you all day? Now let me ask you this. Did you ever become a loyal customer to that business? Would you become a loyal customer to that business if you had the choice? Since you have the answers to these questions, I don't need to go any further. Keep in mind; you can sell scented oils and scented candles in your store simply by using them.

Touching

Customers like to browse. Customers like to touch while they browse. Believe it or not, research proves that touching helps to sell items. You may want to have items opened on display where the customer can feel the texture of a ponytail or mock how the curling iron will perform when they are using it. Customers will not touch unless your items are appealing enough to touch. This goes back to *seeing*.

Tasting

This is a figure of speech. You will want to have good taste in your selections. Not speaking about the items. I am referring to your fixtures and choice of colors. Remember, your store is a commercial location. It is not a residential location. Be careful not to bring too much dedicated colors or arrangements in your business. Ensure your location is appealing to large audience. Use neutral colors and colors that are easy on the eyes. Sometimes we get so passionate about our businesses that we place our emotions in it. But if it doesn't make an impression on the customer's sense, then it won't make an impression on the business' cents!

With serving, you also want to secure. What do I mean? Do not be a close-minded or tunneled-vision servant. Some customers will try to get something for nothing. Some may even attempt (and succeed) at stealing from you. You want to be alert and aware of your surroundings. Make eye contact with your customers at all times. Greet the ones who enter even when serving another customer. This gives off an *alert aura* about you. Once customers know you are paying attention to them whether or not you are right in their presence, they will act accordingly. Keep your store secure by being alert. Yet, you do not want to be overbearing. You do not want be a shadow to the customer, you want to be an assistant to them and sometimes their advisor or expert.

Consistency

It is very important to peak perform. Peak performance is seen as performing at your best level. In your personal life it is recommended by success coaches that you find when your peak performance times are and maximize the use of that time. Let me explain. Some individuals work better at night than in the morning. Others work better in the morning than at night. Some people perform wonderfully in the middle of the day. When an individual finds this time, they want to perform as many tasks as possible during this time as it is more likely for them to do a better job during this time.

Unfortunately, you are not allowed this luxury in running your business. Your business will have to peak perform at all times. You will want your customers able to visit your location at any time and get the same level of excellence. Some businesses get plagued with a reputation of when someone should patronize their location. You tend to hear individuals say, "Go to XYZ Store in the morning cause that night crew is awful." Though you will want to identify your peak time (your time of high traffic volume) and prepare accordingly, you will not want to minimize non-peak times. Bad service to the wrong customer can cause your business some problems. You want to **BE ON TIME EVERYDAY!!!** Don't get caught in the trap of feeling like you are always on time and you are allowed to be late today. Again, bad service to the wrong customer can cause your business some problems. The city of Atlanta's slogan is "Everyday is opening day!" Work under this same principle. Treat everyday like your first day opening. This will keep you consistently working hard and building a reputation of a model business.

When addressing your customers, sir or ma'am is always the standard. It does not matter if the individual is younger than you, wearing dirty clothing, smells bad, acts disrespectfully or is unattractive to you! I will reiterate. Bad service to the wrong customer can cause your business some problems. Your personal feelings were left at the door remember?

Should I set-up a website?

The worldwide web has become and is continuing to be a growing phenomenon. These days, customers are no longer asking IF you have a website but instead WHAT is your website address. It is a proven fact that the web can increase your revenues. The profit margin of selling products over the website is much greater than if you sell in a traditional brick and mortar store. However, the website can become a serious customer service problem if you are not readily equipped to simultaneously conduct business in the brick and mortar AND in the cyber-world. When a business exposes itself to doing business on the web, there comes a wide range of customers with different levels of urgency. When a customer makes a payment via the web and is waiting for their merchandise, they can turn into a thorn in your [business] side. Since their money is gone before the products are received, the on-line customer tends to get uneasy, wouldn't you? Until you establish yourself as credible this is how they will feel. For this reason I only suggest a website once you are totally ready, organized and staffed enough to do so to ensure that your customer service does not suffer.

You will want to treat all customers equally important, whether in-store or on-line. Do not get the attitude of "out of sight, out of mind" and disregard your on-line customers. Your website will require marketing and promotions just like your brick and mortar store does. Your website is simply an extension of your business and operates as a separate business, which requires the attention of any new business. There are companies that can help you get your online store off and running. Do not forego important costs such as website design and hosting for this could yield you an inferior website which could negatively affect your revenues. If you feel you are ready to do e-commerce, then dive in and prepare for substantial profits.

CHAPTER 13
PUTTING YOUR TEAM IN PLACE

Putting Your Team in Place (Chapter 13)

Scheduling

Peak Times

As I previously stated, there are peak times in your business as well as your personal peak time. Let's discuss peak times in business. Different industries possess different peak times. Depending on where your store is located, your peak time may differ from the other businesses around you. Businesses that are located in indoor malls typically share the same peak times, weekends and after 5pm. If your store is in an outdoor strip mall, your peak time may differ from the business sitting right next door to you. Your next-door business neighbor may be a fast-food restaurant that has a peak time of the lunch hour rush Monday through Friday. Then you may have a trucking company whose peak time may be early morning. You will have to determine your peak time based on your business and not the businesses around you. Beauty Supply stores can have early morning, late afternoon, evening or weekend peak times. It depends on the market you are doing business in.

Once you have determined your peak time then you will be able to establish when particular tasks should be handled, such as scheduling, inventory, store maintenance or remodeling. Of course your schedule should reflect a heavier staff during peak times, but keep in mind quality exceeds quantity. Though we as employers would love for all of our employees to be highly competent, this often tends not to be the case. During your peak times, place quality employees in place, rather than just a quantity of employees.

Your employees will want to work as efficient as possible without offending the customer(s). It is not the best tactic to move slowly simply because there is only one customer in the store. Efficiency should always be a top priority plainly because you (or your employees) are not abreast of your customer's schedule and it is not their responsibility to have to express their haste in order for you (or your employees) to speed up their shopping process. How hurried the customer may be is not for the staff to conclude. That is one reason. The other reason is basically, the future is unpredictable. When you may assume that you have time to not be efficient, this situation can change in a matter of minutes. One minute there may be one customer and the next minute there may be 15 or 20, literally. So ensure you train your employees to always move with haste while being efficient.

Conducting Inventory

Your inventory will have to maintained and accounted for. Conducting an inventory can be a very tedious task. Nonetheless, proper inventorying is critical to the success of your business. If you are not conducting an inventory regularly, you can be incurring losses and not even know it. When some items such as glue are sitting on the shelves too long they will sometimes spoil due to inactivity.

Inventorying will also allow you to rotate items that may be at the bottom or at the rear of the stocked items. Theft occurs in stores unbeknownst the staff sometimes and not doing inventory can make you possess false data. Other reasons for conducting inventories are to ensure your inventory is accurate and to identify damages. To make this easier, you may want to designate a "damaged item" section or bin in your store. Use this bin when a customer or employee breaks an item. If you implement a "broke you buy" policy, then you can disregard this bin for customers and utilize it for employees only. These are realities and very valid reasons to conduct inventories, so have your mind conditioned to conduct regular inventories.

When to conduct your inventory is another event you will need to identify. Once you determine the frequency of you conducting inventories, ensure you pick a good time of the day to do so. Allow at least one hour performing the inventory and selecting a time of the day when there is low customer traffic. This will minimize any movement of inventory due to customer sales while performing the inventory.

Your store "maintenance time" should also follow suit with the inventory conduction. Store maintenance should be conducted to keep the store clean and presentable. Keeping a presentable store is crucial to building a loyal customer base. Do not allow yourself to lose the drive to perform at an optimal level. If you become weary, then ensure you find time to relax and recover. Come back to your business with renewed energy. Your habits, behaviors and energy will become contagious to your employees. Remember, "Everyday is Opening Day!"

CHAPTER 14
THE INVENTORY

The Inventory (Chapter 14)

Managing it!

This is your bread and butter. This is what sets you apart from your competitor. This is what pays the bills and keeps your doors opened. With the inventory being so important, you will definitely want to invest the time and money in managing it. Managing your inventory can be a pain-staking task or as simple as 1-2-3! How well are you are able to manage your inventory, depends on how well you set it up to be managed. I have heard several retail store business owners state their frustration in having to watch their inventory and employees with a hawk's eye. This is because of the employees' ability to fraudulently issue products to customer's they know or deeply discount items without authorization. This is an easy chore for an employee who works behind a simple "cash register". A cash register's job is to simply output the user's input. Meaning, whatever the person running the cash register inputs into the cash register, so will the cash register respond with the running total. If you plan to expand your store or have other individuals run your store whether for two minutes or two hours, you will want to have a more sophisticated automated point of sale system. The benefits of having an automated point of sale system are astronomical. It not only helps you to keep a watchful eye over the product, it also eases your tasks and gives you reports that are priceless.

True, this type of system may be pricey but the capabilities of this system are priceless. Following is a list of some of the capabilities of an automated point of sale system.

- ❑   Track Sales
- ❑   Track Inventory
- ❑   Valuates Inventory
- ❑   Tracks the best and worst sales
- ❑   Tracks sales by day, week, month or year
- ❑   Creates its own UPC or skew (product bar code)
- ❑   Tracks Prices
- ❑   Tracks Customers (by name)
- ❑   Tracks Discounts given
- ❑   Tracks last sale of the day
- ❑   Tracks Employees and their sales
- ❑   Establishes Commission Payments
- ❑   Tracks Sales Tax owed

❑ Performs "End-of-the-Day" reports
❑ Restricts the access level of employees

Some points of sale systems do more than others. This list is just an idea of how well you are able to run your store simply because you invested in an automated point of sale system. There are many aspiring owners who prefer to cut costs when it comes to building a business. This is not one of those areas you will want to cut costs in. You will want to develop your business with growth and loss prevention in mind.

In these days, automobiles are manufactured with seat belts and airbags as a standard feature. The manufacturers do not expect the driver to get into a bad car accident but they are equipping the vehicle with the possibility in mind. If the driver gets into an accident, the feature is readily available. You want to exercise the same type of forward thinking, or forethought. This will reduce your time spent on conducting and trying to develop reports on your inventory and/or sales.

Just-In Time

The Japanese created a method of customer fulfillment called "Just-In Time" Inventory. This method was first used by Toyota and has become such a hit that it is now widely used cross-industries by other product fulfillment businesses. Just-In Time (JIT) inventory goes like this. The retailer would develop a reliable portfolio of suppliers/distributors that can get the products to the retailer in the time specified. The time may be one day, a few days a week or more. However, whatever the time specified by the supplier is established to be, their ability to fulfill it to the retailer in that time should NEVER differ. If it does, it erodes the JIT process. Once this time is established, the retailer will order products as soon as the product is needed or will be needed. The retailer will have to know the estimated time of purchase by the customer. This will require the retailer (you) to make a forecast of when the product will be needed.

For example, if you know you sell, on average, 5 straight-edged razors per day and it takes you 4 days to get these razors from your supplier, then you should be placing an order when you have 22-25 razors on hand. In the 4 days it would take for the order to get to your store, you will have sold approximately 20 razors leaving you with enough cushion to not be out of stock when a customer arrives to make a purchase. The most painful words an owner ever has to tell a customer is, "We are out of stock." The most painful words that an owner wants to hear *from* a customer are, "That's all you got?"

Perfecting JIT takes time. There may still be times that you will be out of something simply because one customer placed a large purchase of the same items. It happens. Don't get too wound up over it. The trick is to be consistent overall. You will have isolated incidents.

The objective of JIT was to reduce losses through damages and theft by employees and to also reduce the amount of capital tied up in an inventory. Years ago, I remember working in my uncle's grocery store. In his store, he had two large stock rooms filled with products. True, this ensured he kept stock of items but it also reduced his liquidity. JIT came along and revolutionized the way inventories are handled by having all available products on display, therefore minimizing a sizeable inventory on-hand. This may be a strategy you will want to implement. But keep in mind; JIT is only effective when you are dealing with reliable suppliers, shipping companies and distributors.

Customers typically do not understand supply and demand. If your JIT becomes vulnerable and products are not available, the customer often times does not understand. They know they want a product and they do not care how you get it to the store and if you have a large stock or if you are trying to maximize your liquidity. They want a product, you are a store that sells their product, you should have it is how they tend to think.

Lastly, consider if JIT could work for you. Even without JIT, customers would expect you to order a case of a product for them even though they are the only person ever requesting the product. They would expect you to have a large stock of items that rarely sell. When you do run out of a product be aware that some customers may turn belligerent even to the point of using profanity. But, you remain calm, polite and professional. You have to determine what items are important to order, how much of it or if sub-selling should take place instead. Manage your inventory to the benefit of the business while keeping the customers in mind.

CHAPTER 15
FINANCE
MANAGEMENT

Finance Management (Chapter 15)

Managing the cash flow

I am sure we may agree that cash rules everything around us. Without the cash, everything would stop. Most adults have generated some type of cash flow in their lifetime, whether briefly or extended. The problem many cash strapped persons face is not the ability to generate cash flow but the ability to manage the cash flow. If you have co-workers, you may have heard, "I need a raise. I need to make more money. I am broke." We tend to believe that an increase in revenue is the solution to our problems but we fail to realize the solution to our problems is what raises our cash flow. We look at famous or other high-paid individuals and glorify their positions often wishing to be in the same position. But even the highest paid person can be living check to check. Do not automatically assume that going into business for yourself produces the solution to your financial problems. If you have financial problems and start a business, 9 times out of 10, those problems will follow you into the business and your business will be short-lived. There still will be a cap on how much you can compensate yourself and if you have employees, your compensation will be the last one to be fulfilled. Now that we have cleared up that fallacy, let's move on.

Bank Accounts

There are many different events that occur in your business and you will want to separate them from each other. This way, you will be able to determine what is running right and what is running wrong. In your business you will have payroll to process, reordering of items, tax revenue to submit, new items to purchase, fixed and variable costs to pay, marketing to implement, emergencies to cover, capital expenditures to accumulate and revenue to grow and stockpile, just to name a few. With these different events of the business going on, you do not want to have only one bank account. Imagine if your vehicle only had one red light indicator on the dashboard to alert you of a problem with you car. Well, when this light goes on how will you know specifically what the problem is? This is the similar case. You will want as many dashboard indicators (bank accounts) as possible for each function of your business to alert you or reward you for what is going right or wrong.

Once you have established a bank account for each function then you can better manage the cash flow. You should not be taking from one account to suffice another. If you are, something is not running right with the account that is short. If your sales tax rate is 7%, then 7% of your total gross revenue should be deposited into that account at whatever frequency you determine. I would recommend weekly. This way, when your sales tax worksheet arrives and you fill out your sales revenue information, you can simply enclose the check written from your "tax account" and make your payment then move onto your next order on your agenda. You should not be frazzled trying to determine where the funds will come from to make the payment. This should be the same method for all of your accounts that you will setup.

You will have to establish the percentage of your sales that you would like to be allocated to the different functions, such as marketing, reordering, payroll, growth etc. based on how much of your sales the fixed costs reserves. There is no real rule of thumb for the percentage allocation of your functions. Use your estimated sales revenue as a barometer in depicting your percentages. Marketing can be as little as 2% to 10% of your sales revenue. Bear in mind that the higher the percentage of the marketing, the lower the percentage will be in another function. Also know that you will not be given 100% to begin with as far as determining your percentages. You will have fixed costs that may take up 20% of your sales only leaving you with 80% to work from. You will want to develop a marketing plan that grows and expands to larger audiences as time goes by. You can start with flyer distribution, then direct mailers, moving on to radio and getting to television and cable ads.

If you will have employees making your night deposits, you will also want to setup a "sweep account". This type of account drafts the amount that is in the account and deposits it into another account of your choice daily. This will keep the account number(s) of your operational accounts confidential to you and other authorized personnel.

Let's briefly speak about reordering. You will not have the luxury of plainly choosing a percentage for your reordering budget. If this number is too low, you will constantly find yourself out of items. Be realistic and ensure your revenue is fairly re-invested into the company. Sometimes we can get emotional and tap into the funds for one purpose when those funds serve another purpose.

Set Financial Goals

You will want to also have goals in place. In Chapter 2, Determining Your Market, you were asked to establish your revenue forecast in order to decide whether or not you would be able to sustain your business in your market of choice. Setting financial goals will keep you performing at an optimal level and not getting comfortable in your business' performance. It is important that you continue to raise the bar for you and your employees. This will definitely help you grow your business, generate new ideas, and expand your business into other markets.

Setting up Pay Schedules

Just to reemphasize. You are now the proprietor of your establishment. You are the be all and end all. Many of the decisions that are made and the direction of the business are based on your discernment, decision-making skills, competence, patience and ability. You determine when individuals are paid, to include employees as well as contractors. I have a strict policy never to completely pay contractors for their work until it is totally completed. If they refuse, send them on their way. Contractors come a dime a dozen.

You can also implement a once per month check processing. You can communicate to contractors that may have done emergency or renovation work for you that you process "incidental checks" on the 15th of every month. If they would like to be a part of your business for the long-term, they will often consent to your terms. Exactly how your distributors, service providers, utility companies etc. enforce their terms of operation to you, you also have the power to enforce your terms to others, whether it be employees (within the legal guidelines of the Department of Labor), contractors or other clients.

CHAPTER 16
FINAL WORDS

Final Words (Chapter 16)

We are often ostracized as a race. It is a cliché that Africa-Americans do not stick together. Is it true? Are we so conditioned to being "owned by" that we rarely take ownership? Is it a reason why other races can see the financial benefits in owning or investing in our industries and we cannot? Or is it because of the lack of our resources in our communities that we rarely see opportunities that could be available to us? Perhaps we can do a better job at educating ourselves and understanding the value of owning the plantation instead of just working on the plantation or being a part of the plantation. Whatever the reasons are, we are not properly circulating our consumer buying power within our community. We are leaving the opportunity available for others to capitalize on our items of interest.

It is not wrong for any race to own a stake in the beauty supply industry; however it is wrong for us to not take a larger part in it.

Going into business for oneself is seen to some as the epitome of the American Dream. It can be! It depends on you, the one in control. Many of us African-Americans possess this strong desire to be our own boss, to be in control of our own destiny but many of us do not possess the "know-how" to make this desire a reality. It is going to take hard work and homework. Success is not a secret nor is it automatic. A smaller percentage of individuals succeed and live happy lives meanwhile the numbers of disgruntled individuals who are seeking the way to a quality life are huge.

Take your business serious. Take the customers very serious. Be a steward and servant of the business and the business will do the same to you. Continue to grow in knowledge. It has been said that the application of knowledge is power, not just merely having the knowledge. Subscribe to business periodicals. Know what is going on in your industry. Les Brown once said, "If you want to earn more, you will have to learn more."

You not only want to take control of your destiny! You want to keep it once you have gotten it!

Appendix

Top 15 Reasons to Support a Business In Your Community

1. It helps to build the community's unity, safety and sense of security.

2. Leverages the community's total strength.

3. Creates jobs and minimizes the need for public assistance.

4. Gives economic power and keeps the consumer spending within   the local community.

5. Produces generational wealth.

6. Produces better schools.

7. Generates tax revenue.

8. Appreciates the local market value.

9. Lowers the crime rate.

10. Gives the community enhanced control.

11. Stimulates the mental capacity of the local residents through employment.

12. Offers incentives to be local residents.

13. Keeps the spending power within the local community.

14. Allows the youth to see the importance of entrepreneurship.

15. A strong community has a strong political advantage!

Blacks have become a disenfranchised group plagued with obstacles in America never experienced by others. This has caused this group to become weary from challenges and desperate for piece of the American Dream. Blacks economically supporting their own business communities will aid in the re-establishment of the Black Infrastructure, which we must rebuild one industry at a time. This is what will level the playing field, establish equality and ultimately rid our society of, prejudice, bigotry, and racism.

For consulting or further assistance, write to:

Beauty Supply Institute
P.O. Box 44503
Atlanta, GA 30336
info@beautysupplyinstitute.com

To contact the author go to:

Going Against the Grain Group

www.beautysupplyinstitute.com
www.devinrobinson.com

ORDER FORM

If you would like to order more copies of this title (via mail) please complete the form below and send with check or money order **payable to Going Against the Grain Publications** to the address provided below:

Name: _____

Address: _____

City: _____ State: _____ Zip: _____

Email: _____

"How to Become a Successful Beauty Supply Storeowner"

Of Books _____ x $24.95 = $ _____

Add shipping & handling as indicated:

$5.99 first book: _____ $2.00 each additional book $ _____

Total amount enclosed $ _____

**Books ship immediately upon payment clearance unless temporarily out of stock. There is a $35.00 service fee on ALL returned checks.

Remittance Address:

Beauty Supply Institute

P. O. Box 44503

Atlanta, GA 30336